The Bible For The Clueless But Curious

The Bible For The Clueless But Curious

Nachum Braverman

LEVIATHAN PRESS
BOOKS THAT MAKE A DIFFERENCE

The Bible For The Clueless But Curious
by Nachum Braverman
published by

2505 Summerson Road Baltimore, Maryland 21209
1-800-LEVIATHAN   (410) 653-0300

ISBN 1-881927-17-2

Printed in the United States of America
First Printing / First Edition
Cover and icon design by Staiman Design
Page layout by Fisherman Sam
Distributed to the trade by NBN (800) 462-6420
Distributed to Judaica booksellers by Im Hasefer (718) 377-0047

Group Sales: Leviathan Press books are available to schools, synagogues,
businesses and community organizations at special group rates.
Customized books on a per order basis are also available. Titles include:
Chanukah: Eight Nights of Light, Eight Gifts for the Soul, The One Hour
Purim Primer, Passover Survival Kit, The Survival Kit Family Haggadah,
Rosh Hashanah Yom Kippur Survival Kit, Missiles, Masks And Miracles,
Remember My Soul andThe Death of Cupid: Reclaiming the wisdom of
love, dating, romance and marriage. For information call (410) 653-0300.

Acknowledgments:

First thanks to Uriella Obst who conceived the format for this book.
Uriella, Shimon Apisdorf, Joyce Chernick, David Sacks, Sharon Goldinger, and my father, Robert Braverman commented extensively on the original manuscript. Their criticisms and suggestions immeasurably improved the final product.

Erica Goldberg faithfully typed corrections to the manuscript on her vacation to permit us to finish on deadline.

Yigal Segal edited the Biblical sources.

Shimon Apisdorf created the graphic layout.

Lili Feingold, Rabbi Shalom Denbo, and my wife, Emuna helped edit and proofread the galleys.

Some debts are never repaid. My parents, Robert Braverman and Alice Daniel taught me to think and listen. Rabbi Tom Meyer and Rabbi Noah Weinberg brought me into the covenant of the Jewish People, and Rabbi Weinberg gave me a framework for thinking about the Bible. Rabbi Yaacov Weinberg continually renews my faith in reason.

"A man who isn't married," says the Talmud, "has no wisdom, no help, no joy, no blessing, no atonement, and no good. He isn't called Man." Emuna makes everything possible.

For my children, and for the dispersed of the Children of Israel.

May they speedily come home.

CONTENTS

Chapter Three: Getting Away From It All 39

Chapter Four: Little Children—Little Problems, Big Children—Big Problems 61

INTRODUCTION

Welcome to *The Bible For The Clueless But Curious*.

Maybe the last time you read the Bible was when you had to go to Sunday school. Maybe it was at 1:30 A.M. in a hotel room when you were looking for something to read. Whenever it was, chances are the Bible seemed like gibberish, filled with "thous," "spakes," and "forsooths"—like some weirdo on a street corner, babbling in "tongues."

People used to read the Bible for pleasure. Lincoln read the Bible. Churchill read the Bible. It's the greatest bestseller of all time, the world's first self-help book. You want to know why? That's why I wrote this book.

This book won't talk down at you from the pulpit or make you feel guilty. It won't ask you to accept a bunch of religious dogma on blind faith, and it won't pretend to be the only book you ever need to read if you want to be happy. It will help you understand who's who in the Bible, make sense of what they're talking about, and discover some really useful wisdom.

About This Book

The Bible isn't actually one book but many books bound together. The first big chunk of the Bible is called the Five Books of Moses. It's known as the Pentateuch (penta is Greek for "five," as in "Pentagon"). In Hebrew it's called the Torah, which means "Instructions for Living." The Pentateuch is the most important part of the Bible because everything that comes later depends on it. Since maybe you don't speak Greek or Hebrew, we're just going to call it the Bible.

This book follows the order of the Bible, but you don't have to read it that way. If there's a story that interests you or you want to know what the Bible says about something, look it up and start there. You can also read it straight through from start to finish. Whichever way you do it, enjoy yourself. There's no test at the end.

You'll find that all the well-known stories and important commandments of the Bible are explained in this book. You'll also find sections like:

✦ God's parenting advice
✦ What Cain has in common with the woman who snarled at you in traffic
✦ How come the people in the Bible never got divorced like the rest of us?
✦ How to be insanely happy all the time
✦ How to read the Bible after Darwin
✦ Is God a chauvinist?
✦ Does the Bible say sex is dirty?

How This Book Is Organized

This book is divided into five parts, and each part is broken into chapters.

Part I Genesis / Roots

This part is about the beginning of the world. We'll also meet a lot of people whose names became famous, like Adam, Eve, Noah, Abraham, Sarah, Isaac, Rebecca, Jacob, Rachel, Leah, and Joseph.

Part II Exodus / The Birth Of A Nation

In this part we'll read about the Exodus from Egypt, the Ten Commandments, and the golden calf, as well as Moses, Pharaoh, the burning bush, the stick that turns into a snake, and a cast of thousands of frogs.

Part III Leviticus / Feed And Care For Your Soul

In this part we'll talk about a word that's fallen into disuse lately: "holiness." We'll learn about the holiness of the people, the priests, the body, and even the holiness of time.

Part IV Numbers / Journeying To The Promised Land

The Israelites had all kinds of troubles on their way to the Promised Land, and in this part we'll read about p'agues, rebellions, and wars. If you ever wondered why a trip that should have taken two months took forty years, this is the part for you.

Part V Deuteronomy / A Few Words Before We Part

One month before his death, Moses began to say goodbye to the people, and he told them what he wanted them to remember when he was gone. Think of it as a graduation address or an ethical will.

ICONs Used In This Book

✦ If you don't get the context of what's going on, don't worry, this icon will be there to give you additional background information.

✦ For the spiritual types out there. This icon will alert you to the Bible's messages about God and spirituality.

✦ If in the back of your mind you're saying, "Come on, I don't buy this," be assured, you're not the first to feel that way. This icon will make sense of what seems like nonsense.

✦ Just like the sign says—It's Simple. This icon will present simple, clear explanations of what's going on in the Bible.

✦ When you're wondering why you should care about what the Bible says, this icon will alert you to important wisdom for living being taught.

✦ This icon alerts you to insights into life's most important relationships.

✦ *To be, or not to be …*

This icon highlights quotes whose wisdom complements the Bible's message.

✦ When you feel the Bible's wisdom is locked away in concepts too deep for the average Joe—this icon explains and illustrates the most complex ideas.

✦ "Just gimme the facts!" That's exactly what you'll get when you see this icon.

✦ Biblical Sources

Whenever you see type that looks like this, it means that the Bible is either being quoted or that I'm giving you the gist of the story—often with my own gloss on the Bible's language.

(Biblical quotes will be followed by a page and verse reference. I chose <u>The Stone Edition of The Chumash</u> (that's Hebrew for Bible) published by Mesorah Publications—and you should too.)

Contacting The Author

You can contact me by e-mail at: RabbiNB@aol.com

Where To Go From Here

Reading the Bible for the first time is an adventure into a strange and wonderful new world. Like all adventures, it can be exciting and also a little scary. Like all adventures, this one starts "In the beginning … "

PART I

Genesis
Roots

The first book of the Bible is the book of Genesis. Genesis means "root" or "source."

Our roots tell us where our parents came from and what kind of people they were. People like to know about their roots because it helps them understand who they are and how they got to be that way.

If you want to understand what the Bible says about where the world came from, or why the world is the way it is, start reading here. If you think no one who took tenth grade biology can take the Bible seriously, you're also in the right place to start.

CHAPTER 1

Where Do We Come From
And Who Cares?

Everyone thinks there's something special about being alive and wants to know how life began. Science does a good job of explaining some things, but there are many important questions science can't answer. Science tells us how long life has been around but not the *meaning* of being alive. Science helps us understand what causes illness and which medicines bring health, but it doesn't address questions like whether our lives have purpose, if we have a soul, or what happens when we die. The Book of Genesis is about the questions science can't answer. It's about where we came from, where we're going, and why we should care.

Creation

> *The Bible says God created the world in seven days.*
> *The seven days went like this:*

Day 1: *Light and darkness*
Day 2: *Sky*
Day 3: *Sea, dry land, and plants*
Day 4: *Sun, moon, and stars*
Day 5: *Birds and fishes*
Day 6: *Animals and Human beings*
Day 7: *Rest and Contemplation*

(Genesis 1:1-2:3; pp. 3-11)

Just Who Or What Is God, And What Does He Want?

The Bible speaks of God in three ways:

1. God *created* our world (and everything else)

Because God made the world, everything in the world helps us understand who God is.

If you went into the house of a man you didn't know, you could learn a lot about him by looking at his home. You'd learn how he likes to spend his time, what he likes to eat and, whether he reads or watches television. You might come to feel you know him, even without meeting him. That's the way creation works. Because God made it, everything in the world teaches us about God. God made the world so we could know Him, even though we haven't met him.

2. God *sustains* the world.

God's relationship with the world is different from that of most creators and their creations. The couch in your living room keeps standing there, even though the carpenter who made it has long since forgotten about it. By contrast, imagine a girl riding a bicycle by the beach. Now think about something else. What happens to the girl? As soon as you divert your attention—blip—the girl on the bike is gone. The *world* is like the girl on the bike in your mind, not like the couch. God *sustains* the world by thinking about it.

3. God *supervises* the world.

G od keeps checking to see how the world is going. He fixes and tinkers with it, He cares about us, and He hears our prayers.

W hy does God do all this? Because He loves us.

If He's God, Who's She?

G od isn't a he or a she. The Bible is written so we can understand it. The Bible wants us to know God loves us and wants a relationship with us. If the Bible called God "it," we'd be left feeling God was some kind of uncaring, impersonal machine.

Speaking of God, Or Vice-Versa

G od doesn't speak the way you and I do. God doesn't have a mouth (or hands or feet) "God spoke" means God expressed the will for something to happen, and so it did. (Don't you wish you could do that?)

Reading the Bible After Darwin

S ome scientists believe man evolved from an ape-like ancestor over millions of years. The Bible says God created the world in seven days. Many people think you can believe one or the other, but not both.

It isn't as bad as it seems.

Back in the twelfth century, long before anyone heard of Darwin, scholars pointed out that in the Bible life seems to, how can I say this, "evolve." First there is life in the sea, then simple life on earth, and finally people. But the Bible says these things didn't happen by accident. God made them happen. Maybe the way God made them happen was by using some form of evolution.

> *Nature is miracles we're used to.*
>
> Nachmanides, 11th century

What about the seven days? That's a lot less than the 4 1/2 billion years carbon dating suggests our world has been around.

Many people believe the Bible's "days" aren't twenty-four hour days. For one thing, the sun and moon weren't created until the fourth day—so days one through three probably weren't "days" as we think of them. What the Bible is *really* telling us, is that the world was made in seven "periods," but each period could have been millions of years long. (Maybe the fifth day was the Jurassic period.)

You may have heard people say that the world is 5758 years old (give or take a few years). This is not the number of years since creation. It is the number of years since Adam, the first man with a *soul*.

People care whether the world evolved or whether God made the world because it changes the way we think about ourselves. It seems a lot more special to have been created by God than to be a later model ape. Think about this:

If there is no difference between people and animals, why should we treat people differently from animals? When I'm hungry or want a nice watchband, I can kill a cow and tan its hide. Is there any reason not to make a watchband out of human skin? The Bible says the reason you can't is that people aren't just animals. A person has a soul (more about the soul later).

If people are just animals, there's no reason to expect them to act better than animals. When a tiger kills and eats someone it isn't evil—it's just doing what tigers do. And although people can be crueler than animals, we also expect them to be much better and to control their aggression and their appetites. Try saying this to a tiger: "Hey, I don't care how much you want that gazelle. You can't grab it off your sister's plate."

Who Is That Talking Snake, And What's He Doing In My Garden?

The first people were Adam and Eve.
After God creates them, He puts Adam and Eve in the Garden of Eden. (Eden means "pleasure.") Their job is to take care of the Garden and to eat its fruit. The one thing prohibited was to eat fruit from the Tree of Knowledge.
God sends a snake to Adam and Eve to test them.
The snake's job is to make eating from the Tree of Knowledge seem very appealing. Here's how he did it:
Snake: (played by Jack Nicholson) "Hey, this is some set-up you have here in the Garden. Too bad God's got you on such a short leash you can't enjoy it."

Eve: (played by Kate Winslet) "Oh no. God's very good to us. We
can eat the fruit of all the trees here, except the Tree of Knowledge.
If we eat that one, we'll die."
Snake: "But that's the best one! That's the one that makes you like
God. What do you want to stand around here and be God's choir for?
And hey, maybe you'll die. But maybe you won't. C'mon,
let me show you how pretty this fruit is."
Eve eats, and the rest is history.

(Genesis 3:1-7; pp. 15-17)

Why wouldn't God want Adam and Eve to have knowledge? In the Bible, the word "knowledge" doesn't mean the same as "wisdom." It means something much more passionate and intimate. That's why when two people have sexual relations, the Bible says "he knew her." A biologist or botanist can *study* a peach, but you don't *know* a peach until you eat it. After Adam and Eve eat fruit from the Tree of Knowledge, they no longer react to moral choices in an objective, dispassionate way. Suddenly they are intimately concerned about the personal consequences of their choices—deciding what *feels* good, rather than deciding what makes sense. Think of this example: I know smoking causes cancer. I see the warning on the label. I know people who have died of cancer. But I feel like smoking. I know there's a risk, but maybe I'll be lucky, and anyway I like the taste.

Why do people do things they know don't make sense? Blame it on Adam and Eve.

Tough Love

After Adam and Eve eat from the Tree of Knowledge, God asks one
of the great innocent questions of all time.
"Tell me," he says, "Did you eat from that tree I told you
not to eat from?"

(Genesis 3:11, p. 17)

Parenting Tip from God, the master parent: Never start with an accusation. Start with a question. That way you encourage your kids to take responsibility for themselves and their actions.

Raise 'em Right

But of course, Adam and Eve don't fess up. Instead, Adam blames Eve and Eve blames the snake. The snake has no one left to blame. Then a few things happen, none of them pleasant:
✦ Eve is punished with the pain of bearing and raising children. (If you don't think dealing with your kid's adolescence is a punishment, you probably don't have kids.)
✦ Eve is told she'll have to wait for Adam to take the lead in marital relations. (Don't blame me, I'm just telling you what it says.)
✦ Adam is told he'll have to "earn bread by the sweat of his brow."
✦Adam and Eve become mortal.

(Genesis 3:12-22; pp. 17-19)

What's the point of all this?

God doesn't punish Adam and Eve because He hates them. He punishes them because He *loves* them, and He wants them to understand what they've done wrong.

Consequences are *good* for us, because they make us responsible for ourselves. Imagine how hard you'd work in school if there were no grades or tests and no one knew whether you went to class or not. Part of the reason communism failed is that when there's no reward for excellence and no consequence for failure, everyone winds up the same—mediocre. Even death is good because it makes us think about what we really want to do with our lives.

Raise 'em Right

If you want to mess your kids up really good, never punish them. It's a guarantee they'll turn into total monsters. If you want your kids to be the kind of people you'd choose to spend the afternoon with, you need to balance love, support, and approval on the one hand, and discipline on the other.

To top it all off, God throws Adam and Eve out of the Garden of Eden.

(Genesis 3:24; p. 19)

Think of it as tough love.

The Kids Start Fighting

Things go on from bad to worse. Adam and Eve have two children: Cain and Abel. When harvest time comes, Cain and Abel bring offerings to God as a way of giving thanks.
Abel offers "the first and fattest sheep of his flock,"
but Cain decides that's overdoing the gratitude thing, and he gives some of his poorer crops. God isn't very impressed with this, and He tells Cain so. Cain becomes depressed, and decides to take it out on Abel (God being too tough, and too far away to fight with). Cain picks a fight with Abel about which one of them God loves more, and then Cain kills him.
In His most innocent voice, God asks Cain: "What happened to your brother Abel?"
"I don't know," says Cain. "Am I my brother's keeper?"

(Genesis 4:1-9; pp. 19-21)

The Bible teaches that it doesn't matter what, or how much we have. It matters whether we *take pleasure* in what we have. Right now, for example, you can walk, talk, and think—blessings you probably wouldn't trade for a million dollars each but probably all blessings you've learned to take for granted. But if you can take for granted being able to see or speak, what do you think you'll achieve or acquire in your life that you *won't* take for granted?

The way to appreciate and enjoy the abilities we have (like being able to see) is to think of them as gifts from God and to thank Him for them. That's why Cain and Abel give offerings to God.

What Cain has in common with the woman who snarled at you in traffic:

Violence has nothing to do with the victim. Cain commits murder because he's depressed and angry. He could think about the failures of his own life, and try to fix them, but that would take a lot of work. It's easier to blame Abel.

Blaming your problems on others is a cheap way to avoid the difficulty of change and growth. In today's society, it sometimes seems no one wants to accept responsibility for his behavior. In one particularly silly (but true) illustration of this, a woman recently bought a cup of coffee from McDonald's, put the cup between her legs, and drove off. When the coffee spilled and burned her, she sued McDonald's!

Not accepting responsibility is the key to violence in families as well. A husband comes home frustrated at the end of a difficult day. He's looking for someone to blame. Who's around to hurt? His wife and kids! Why is his frustrating day their fault? It isn't of course, but within a few minutes of arriving home, some provocation arises, and he lets them have it.

Strange Names of Dead People

*After Cain and Abel, the Bible lists the ten generations
from Adam to Noah. They are*:

Adam	Yered
Seth	Chanoch
Enosh	Metushelach
Kenaan	Lemech
Mehalalel	Noah

(Genesis 4:25-5:32; pp. 23-27)

Who *are* all these people, and why do they have such unpronounceable names?

Most of these people are pretty bad. Their names mean things like: "may God be blotted out" (Mehalalel) and "rebellion against God" (Yered). The Bible tells us that the way things started with Adam, Eve, and Cain, is the way things kept going.

The only exception to this sorry downward path is Enosh. The Bible says "Enosh walked with God." He was a shoemaker, and as he made shoes, he told himself, "I want these shoes to last and protect the feet of the people who wear them."

There are two ways to approach work. One way is to see doing a job as the means and making money as the goal. The other is to see doing a job as the goal, and making money as the reward for a job well done. If you approach work the second way, you'll walk with God. (You may also ultimately do better in business. For example, many people attribute the decline of the American auto industry to Detroit's emphasis on making money, while the Japanese focused on making cars people would want to drive.)

CHAPTER 2

A Good Man Is Hard To Find

After Cain and Abel, things go from bad to worse. Murder and robbery become commonplace. Leaders are corrupt, and use their power for personal pleasure and profit. People become cynical, and right and wrong are defined by what you can get away with. (Of course, today things are very different. Most people have enough moral sensitivity not to smoke in public!)

God eventually decides enough is enough and it's time to start over. In the entire world, the only decent people are Noah and his family.

(Genesis 6:1-8; pp. 27-29)

Noah Tries Boating

God tells Noah to build a really big boat, called an ark. The ark has three floors:

One for Noah and his family, one for the animals, and one for their garbage (very practical).

God tells Noah to take into the ark:

✦ *Seven pairs of each of the clean animals; animals that will later be used for sacrifices. (Don't worry, we'll talk about sacrifices later.)*

✦ *Two pairs of each of the unclean animals: wolverines, bats, cobras, etc.*

✦ *His three children—Shem, Ham, and Yefes—and their wives.*

(Genesis 6:9-19; pp. 31-33)

Uh Noah, the Sea Is Two Thousand Miles Away

Noah seems very odd to people, building his ark out in Kansas (or wherever he is), but that is part of the point. God wants people to ask Noah why he needs a boat in the middle of the Great Plains, so Noah can have the opportunity to warn them about God's plan to destroy the world. God hopes they will take this warning to heart and change their behavior. God doesn't want to destroy the world.
He wants people to change.

(Genesis 6:9-22; pp. 31-33)

When I was eighteen, I had a screaming fight with my Dad and stormed out of the house. It was three months before I cooled down enough to go home. Early one morning, I knocked on my parents' door, and my Dad opened it.

"I've missed you terribly," my Dad said. "I'm so glad you've come home."

God doesn't expect us to be perfect, and He certainly takes no joy in hurting us. He expects us to take responsibility for our mistakes and to change. In this respect, God is a lot like my Dad, or maybe the other way around.

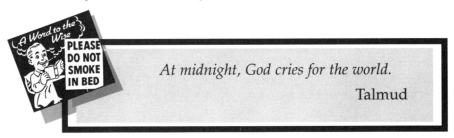

At midnight, God cries for the world.
Talmud

One hundred and twenty years pass from the time Noah starts building the ark until the flood comes. Even once the rain starts, it begins gently. God is very patient. Until the last moment, He hopes people will realize how bad things are and change.

(Genesis 7:6-16; pp. 33-35)

When your kids make mistakes, don't be too quick to punish them. Think of ways to help them realize their mistakes and to change.

Raise 'em Right

When you *do* have to punish your children, it's important to let them know how sad it makes you. You don't want them to think you enjoy your power over them. Hurting the people you love most is something you do reluctantly, and only because you know you need to do it, for *their* good.

Would *You* Listen To a Guy With a Sign Saying the World Was Going To End?

The Bible says there is such a thing as prophecy, which means hearing God speak. For the moment, take at face value that Noah hears God speak, and that he doesn't think it is his neighbor playing a practical joke on him.

The people in Noah's time also know there are prophets, and Noah, being wise and good, seems like a reasonable candidate. In addition, this isn't too long after Adam, so people know about God and the expectations He has of His creation.

If God Wants the World Saved, Why Doesn't *He* Build the Ark?

Noah is the best of his generation. He sees how bad the people around him are, and he doesn't act like them. On the other hand, Noah isn't *that* good. Although he keeps his own nose clean, he doesn't do anything to try to improve the world around him. God tells Noah to build the ark so Noah would understand he had to take responsibility for others to deserve being saved himself.

This AFFECTS YOU

The Bible teaches that to be a good person, it isn't enough not to hurt anyone; you have to actively try to make the world better.

Rainy Days

No one pays much attention to this big boat Noah is building, and the rain begins. It rains for forty days and forty nights, until the whole world is covered with water.
The flood covers the earth for an entire year.
During the year in the ark, Noah and his wife are prohibited from having sexual relations.

(Genesis 7:11-24; pp. 35-37)

Enjoying yourself while people all around you are suffering (in this case drowning), makes you callous.

Here's the kind of thing the Bible might be warning against:

"Anything in the paper, honey?"

"Nah, just a million people massacred in Rwanda. You want to go down to the mall? There's a sale on."

At the end of the year, Noah opens the ark's window and sends out a bird to discover if the waters of the flood have subsided.
First he sends out a raven, but the raven just flies round and round the ark.
Then he sends a dove. The first time, the dove finds no dry land and returns to the ark. Then Noah sends the dove a second time, and when it returns, it brings an olive branch in its mouth. The third time Noah sends out the dove it doesn't return, and Noah knows the flood is over.

(Genesis 8:6-14; pp. 37-39)

The dove with an olive branch in its mouth is a sign to Noah that the violence and destruction covering the earth has abated. It has become the universal symbol of peace.

Boy It's Good To Get Out

Noah and his family leave the ark. Since he's just seen the world destroyed, Noah is afraid to start over. God promises him the world will never again be destroyed through flood. (Note, however, that still leaves God lots of options—like fire, hurricanes, earthquakes, pestilence, or nuclear catastrophe. Only floods are off the table.) God puts the rainbow in the sky as a symbol and reminder of this promise.

(Genesis 8:18-9:17; pp. 39-43)

Now Listen Up

God gives Noah seven commandments that apply to the entire world—Jew and Gentile alike.

Because the whole world is descended from Noah (remember, no one else survived the flood) these commandments are called the Seven Noahide commands. They are:

1. Don't murder.
2. Don't steal.
3. Don't commit adultery.
4. Don't worship idols.
5. Don't blaspheme (curse God).
6. Don't eat limbs off live animals. (I know you don't think this is a temptation, but apparently it was a problem.)
7. Set up a court system, and administer justice.

Noah Has a Bit Too Much To Drink

Overwhelmed by the destruction he has witnessed, Noah plants a vineyard. When the crop is harvested, Noah becomes drunk. He lies in his tent, exposed and naked.

*Noah's youngest son, Ham, sees Noah drunk and ridicules him.
Then Shem and Yefes cover Noah with a cloak to protect him from
shame. Noah awakens, realizes what has happened, and curses the
descendants of Ham. (This is your clue that Ham's disrespect for his
father was a big mistake.)*

(Genesis 9:20-27; pp. 43-45)

Today it's popular for homes to be run democratically. Mom gets a vote, Dad gets a vote, and each of the kids gets a vote. If Mom and Dad get outvoted, well, they just have to accept the will of the people.

Raise 'em Right

By contrast, the Bible teaches that children's respect and deference to their parents is crucial *for the kids*. Through obedience to their parents, children learn boundaries. Without boundaries, kids can't learn self-discipline.

A Tall Building

*The flood leaves Noah's descendants frightened and vulnerable. To
protect themselves against similar "acts of God" in the future, they
band together to build a tall tower toward heaven. God interferes by
making them all speak different languages. (Babel in Hebrew means
mixed up, hence the tower of Babel.) Because they are unable to
communicate, they are forced to abandon building the tower, and then
they scatter around the world.*

(Genesis 11:1-9; p. 49)

Death is so frightening we try to escape it. We get plastic surgery and dress in ways that make us look young. We look for accomplishments we'll be remembered for. Some people spray-paint their name on freeway overpasses. Some try to become rich, powerful, or famous. Some write books! At times, people are even willing to surrender their freedom to participate in something they think will offer them vicarious immortality. For the chance to be part of his "Thousand Year Reich," most Germans and Austrians welcomed Hitler's dictatorship with delirious joy.

CHAPTER 3

Getting Away From It All

Abram Sets Out On His Own

The rest of the Bible is about the descendants of a man named Abram. (If you're confused because you thought his name was Abraham, stay tuned. God changes his name later.) Abram isn't called a "Jew." He is called a "Hebrew," which means someone who stands alone, and apart from the rest of the world. Abram's way of seeing life is so unique he stands alone.

Abram lives in a place called Charan. Everyone around him worships idols, which seems so silly, it's hard for us to understand. But think of it like worshipping love, or success, or good health. These are all good and important, but if you planned your whole life around building big biceps that would be idolatry.

Abram decides God must have created the world because it is too complicated and beautiful to have happened by accident. (Believing the world happened by chance is sort of like believing my wristwatch accidentally fell together in a shoebox full of gears and springs.)

> God says to Abram: "Go for yourself from your land,
> from your relatives, and from your father's house
> to the land that I will show you.
> And I will make you into a great nation.
> I will bless you, and make your name great,
> and you will be a blessing … all the families of the earth
> shall bless themselves by you."
>
> (Genesis 12:1-3; p. 55)

Where we live and how the people around us behave makes a big impact on how *we* think and behave. If people around us think powdered wigs and petticoats are stylish, we'll probably think so too.

If our friends own slaves or believe in the divine right of kings, chances are we'll agree, and if people around us think religion is a joke and drugs are cool, chances are we'll agree with that too. The first thing God tells Abram is that he has to become independent. And to become independent, he has to move away from home. (Sound familiar?)

Dr. Stanley Milgrom once did an experiment at Yale University that became very famous. Milgrom brought two people into his laboratory; let's call them Harry and Jack. (Unbeknownst to Harry, Jack was really Milgrom's partner.) Milgrom told them they would participate in an experiment to explore how punishment affects learning.

Dr Milgrom: "Harry, I'm going to take Jack into this little room over here and attach an electrode to his arm. He's going to have fifteen minutes to memorize a list of words. Then you'll test him on them. Every time Jack makes a mistake, you're going to give him a shock. The shock will be a little stronger each time."

Jack: "I have a bad heart. This isn't going to hurt me, is it?"

Milgrom: "It's all in the interest of science. Don't worry."

The experiment starts and Jack makes a mistake.

Milgrom: "O.K., Harry, give Jack a shock."

Jack: "Ouch!"

Harry: "You know, that *did* hurt him. Maybe we shouldn't do this."

Milgrom: "Harry, the experiment requires that you go on. Please continue."

The experiment continues. Jack starts screaming and pounding on the walls. The dial eventually indicates that Harry is giving Jack lethal shocks, Jack becomes totally silent. Harry is visibly upset, but goes on giving the shocks anyway, *past the point where he believes he's killed Jack.*

Milgrom's experiment showed it isn't necessary to be vicious, cruel, or sadistic to put people into gas chambers. You can be completely normal but just not independent enough to ask whether what you're being asked to do is right or wrong.

"Independence of conscience" is an important part of how Abram's descendants define themselves.

Sarai Gets Nabbed

> *Abram leaves Charan, and comes to Canaan together with his wife, Sarai, and his nephew, Lot. God appears to Abram and says, "I will give this land to your descendants."*
> *Soon after, there is a bad famine, and Abram and his family go to Egypt looking for food.*

(Genesis 12:6-10; p. 57)

Sarai's name is later changed to Sara. We'll hear more about Lot later too. The Land of Canaan is known later as the Land of Israel. It's called "Canaan" after the tribes that live there—descendants of Ham's son, Canaan.

If frustration sometimes tests your faith, you can take comfort from Abram. Just after God promised to make Abram great, rich, and famous, he has to flee to Egypt, hungry and penniless. Maintaining hope and trust in God in the face of disappointment is an important part of being great.

A Word to the Wise

PLEASE DO NOT SMOKE IN BED

Hope is not the same thing as optimism. [Hope] is not the conviction that something will turn out well, but the certainty that something makes sense, regardless of how it turns out.

Vaclav Havel, Disturbing the Peace

Egypt at the time is not a place of strong law and order. A beautiful woman is at risk of being kidnapped or raped. And if she's married, her husband risks being murdered. Abram and Sarai pretend to be brother and sister. Sarai is kidnapped and she's taken to Pharaoh to be his concubine. (That's a step down from a wife—it's not good.)
God intervenes and strikes Pharaoh and his house with plagues until Pharaoh releases Sarai unharmed. Frightened and guilty, Pharaoh showers Abram and Sarai with gifts, and then together with Lot, they return to Canaan.

(Genesis 12:10-13:4; pp. 57-59)

HELP! I Need More Info

One of the interesting aspects of this story is that it's outline is repeated four hundred years later in the story of the Hebrews' slavery in Egypt: famine forces the Hebrews to take refuge in Egypt. There, they become enslaved by Pharaoh. God afflicts the Egyptians with plagues until Pharaoh releases the Israelites. The Israelites return to Canaan loaded with gold and silver.

The idea that the actions of the forefathers create the future of their descendants runs throughout the Book of Genesis. A simple way of putting it is, "as a twig is bent, so grows the tree."

More Fighting

Remember Abram's nephew, Lot? Lot's moral principles are not the highest. Lot lets his sheep pasture in other people's fields, and he justifies this by saying: "God promised the land of Israel to Abram. Since I am Abram's only heir it will eventually all belong to me, so what I'm doing isn't really stealing."

Disgusted, Abram asks Lot to move away.
Lot goes away and lives in Sodom, a luxurious and lovely city by
what is now called the Dead Sea. The residents have some unlovely
habits, like robbing and killing travelers. But this doesn't deter Lot.
He wants the backyard.

(Genesis 13:5-13; pp. 59-61)

I'm going to quote the Talmud a lot. We'll discuss it in some depth when we get to the Ten Commandments and talk about "the oral law." For the moment, think of the Talmud as an oral tradition of the Bible's deeper meaning.

When you choose where to live, don't consider just the school district and the taxes. Think about the people that you're going to live near because your children are going to wind up a whole lot like them. (See also "Abram sets out on his own.")

There are four characters among people:

The good man says, "what's mine is yours,
and what's yours is yours."

The evil man says, "what's mine is mine,
and what's yours is mine."

The fool says, "What's mine is yours and what's yours is mine."

"What's mine is mine, and what's yours is yours."—This
institutionalized selfishness, sort of "don't bother me and I
won't bother you," this is the character of Sodom.

Ethics of the Fathers

That's Friendship

Shortly after Lot arrives in Sodom, the city is attacked, and Lot is carried off hostage. Though Abram dislikes Lot, he feels loyalty demands he risk his life to save him.

(Genesis 14:1-16; pp. 61-65)

One day a man pulls his son aside and asks how many friends he has.

"A great many," the son says. "Ten or a dozen at least."

Dubious, his father suggests a test.

"Slaughter a lamb and put it in a bag. Bring it to the home of one of your friends in the middle of the night. Tell him you accidentally killed a man in a barroom, and ask him to help you bury the body."

A week later the son returns distraught, and friendless.

"Do *you* have any friends?" he asks his father.

"I have a half-friend," the father tells him. "Go to Chaim with the same story and see what happens."

The son returns to report Chaim has helped him bury the body.

"But why do you say he's only a *half*-friend," he asks.

"What did he say when you first came to his door?"

"He said he really shouldn't help me, but that since I'm your son he didn't have a choice."

"That's why he's only *half* a friend. I never had a *whole* friend, but I'll tell you a story I heard about real friends.

Once there were two men who were friends. One of them lived in Damascus while the other lived in Jerusalem. When the man from Jerusalem was in Damascus on business, he was arrested, convicted of spying and sentenced to die. At his trial he implored the king:

'I am a merchant with ships around the world, and many people are dependent on me for their livelihood. Give me one month to put my affairs in order. Then I will return and you can put me to death.'

The king refused.

'I'm his guarantor,' the friend exclaimed. 'Imprison me in his place, and if he doesn't return, execute me in his place.'

The king acceded and the convicted man left.

At the end of the month the condemned man was delayed on his return, and his friend was taken out to die. At the last moment the spy burst into the square shouting:

'Wait! Stop the execution! I am the man condemned to die!'

But his friend, already on the block, demurred.

'You are too late, and now I am the one who must die.'

'But I'm the spy,' the other said, and they began to argue which one of them should die. Uncertain what to do, the executioner took both men before the king.

'You two are such good friends I'll spare both of you,' said the King 'on condition you make me a third friend.'

"If two men are true friends, the Almighty makes himself the third friend."

—Story heard from Rabbi Weinberg

Thanks, But No Thanks

Abram rescues Lot and others captured with him. The King of Sodom tries to reward Abram.
"Thanks," says Abram, "but I can't afford to be indebted to you."

(Genesis 14:21-24; p. 65)

Every gift received creates a debt. If you're not going to want to pay the debt, don't accept the present.

Promises To Keep

When the war is over, Abram returns home. Abram and Sarai are long past the age of bearing children. God appears to Abram and makes him two promises. The first promise is that Abram and Sarai will have children ("as innumerable as the stars of the heavens" is God's phrase—it means lots). The second promise is that Abram's descendants will become a great nation and inherit the Land of Israel.

(Genesis 15:1-7; p. 67)

Abram accepts God's promise of children, but he is dubious of the promise his descendants will inherit the land. Possession of the land of Israel will depend on the choices of tens of generations over hundreds of years. What if his children decide they'd rather live in Great Neck?

God makes a covenant with Abram. (A covenant is like a contract.) God guarantees there will be a nation of Israel and that his descendants will eventually inherit the Promised Land.

(Genesis 15:9-21; pp. 67-71)

There is a subtle balance between personal responsibility and dependence on God. We'll talk much more about this when we talk about the Exodus. For now, let's just say that if you know God will help you, you can have a much loftier vision of what's possible.

Don't Try This At Home!

Despite God's promise, Abram and Sarai have no kids. Sarai has a servant named Hagar. She reasons that if Abram has a child with Hagar, she (Sarai) can raise the child as her own. She also believes this selflessness on her part will count in her favor with God. (It was one of those things that seems like a good idea at the time. Later, you say to yourself, "what was I thinking?!")

Hagar becomes pregnant, but predictably enough, it doesn't work out so well. Hagar lords it over Sarai. Sarai becomes jealous and yells at Abram. Abram wishes he were somewhere else.

(Genesis 16:1-6; p. 71)

The Bible is brutally honest about the strengths and weaknesses of the patriarchs and matriarchs. Some wit once said, "The Bible could *only* have been written by God, because if it *wasn't*, it was written by an anti-Semite."

Remember the Scene In Pinocchio When Wild Boys Turn Into Donkeys?

God tells Hagar to name her son Ishmael, which means "God has heard." God also tells Hagar that Ishmael will be a wild donkey of a man, dominated by his appetites, his passions, and his resentments.

(Genesis 16:11-12; pp. 71-73)

The Jews and the Arabs share a tradition that Ishmael is the ancestor of the Arab peoples.

You Want Me to Do *What*?

God appears to Abram and offers to make another covenant with him. The last covenant guaranteed that Abram would have descendants who would inherit the land of Canaan. This covenant commits God to an intimate relationship with those descendants (as though your Dad said, "Wherever you go, I will always love you and look out for you"). As a sign of Abram's acceptance of the deal, God asks Abram to circumcise himself and all his descendants. This is called bris milah. (Bris means "covenant." Milah means "cut.") Because of this bris, Abram's descendants are called "the children of the covenant," or in Hebrew, b'nai brith.

(Genesis 17:1-14; pp. 73-75)

This AFFECTS YOU

A human being is a body and a soul.

We aren't meant to be ascetics or to deny our bodies pleasure. But the ideal relationship between body and soul is like the relationship between a horse and rider. Like a horse, the body has power and drive to get you where you want to go, but if it hasn't been taught to respond to the soul's commands, the body's appetites can get you killed. (Using the power of the body's drive to reach for higher goals is called "sublimation.")

Circumcision symbolizes our determination to channel our deepest passions toward higher ends.

You Look To Me Like An Abraham

At the time of this second covenant, God changes Abram's name to Abraham. He changes Sarai's name to Sarah.

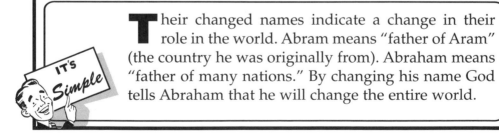

Their changed names indicate a change in their role in the world. Abram means "father of Aram" (the country he was originally from). Abraham means "father of many nations." By changing his name God tells Abraham that he will change the entire world.

God Drops By

*Abraham is circumcised at ninety-nine years of age. While Abraham
is recuperating, God appears to him.*

(Genesis 18:1; p. 79)

We learn from this passage that there is a *mitzvah* to visit the sick. Many people think of a *mitzvah* as a good deed, like, "Eat the leftover cookies. It's a *mitzvah*." Actually, a mitzvah is a commandment—something we need to do. As we'll see, the Ten Commandments are not God's ten suggestions.

*If you visit the sick, you take away one
sixtieth of their illness.*

Talmud

Pardon Me, But Something Really Important Has Come Up

*While talking with God, Abraham looks up and sees three strangers
straggling down the road. Interrupting his conversation, he runs out,
and grabs the travelers. "Let me just bring you some bread and water,"
he says to them. He tells Sarah to make some bread. He slaughters a
calf, brings the travelers into his tent, and serves them their meal.*

(Genesis 18:1-8; p. 79)

Practicing kindness is even more important than receiving prophecy. When you care for other people, you're being *like* God.

No matter how hard you try, you can't understand your parents until you become a parent yourself. We similarly can't grasp God's love for us until we care for others.

If you live for yourself, the world is a cold and unfriendly place. It seems impossible to believe there is a God who cares for us. When you give to others, the world is suddenly full of God's loving embrace. If you're bitter or sad, giving to others is the very best medicine possible.

Abraham promises his guests bread and water, but he delivers a feast. Most people promise a lot and deliver little. Really good people say little and do much.

Ever Wish You Could Do This to Your Neighbors?

The three travelers Abraham is feeding turn out to be angels (think of them as God's FedEx system). One of the angels brings Abraham the message that Sarah will soon conceive and bear a child.
Sarah is ninety at the time.
She is a little surprised by this news, and she laughs,
"How can we have a child? Abraham and I are much too old!"
God asks Abraham why Sarah said she was too old to have a child,
(but God doesn't mention to Abraham that Sarah also thinks Abraham is too old.)
(Genesis 18:9-15; p. 81)

While lying is generally a bad idea, the Bible permits lying, or as here, telling just part of the truth, to spare people's feelings and to preserve peace.

When the angels leave, God says, "Abraham has accepted responsibility to teach the world about kindness and justice. I have to explain to him how I run my world." Then God tells Abraham he is about to destroy the cities of Sodom and Gomorrah.

(Genesis 18:17-21; pp. 81-83)

While you may not explain your business strategy to your secretary, you have to explain it to your partner. God says, in effect, "Abraham accepts responsibility to perfect the world. That makes him my partner."

Abraham objects to God's plan to destroy Sodom.
He argues that good people will be killed along with the bad.
He negotiates an agreement with God: Sodom and Gomorrah will be spared if there are ten good people in the cities.

(Genesis 18:23-33; pp. 83-85)

Ten is a special number in the Bible (Ten plagues, Ten Commandments). Communal prayer requires ten men, which is another way of saying that ten men create a *community*. Abraham acknowledges no individual can maintain his own principles amidst the depraved morals of Sodom. But he argues that a community of good people within Sodom could maintain itself, and might even eventually change the city.

A Bad Place To Run Out of Gas

Still in human guise, the angels arrive in Sodom and meet Lot, now mayor of Sodom. A holy man he's not, but Lot grew up in Abraham's house. He knows the importance of hospitality, and he invites the travelers to his home. The people of Sodom don't like hospitality. They don't want poor people coming to Sodom, loitering on street corners, and depressing property values. They have a law against charity. When they hear Lot has taken travelers into his home, the people of Sodom go to his house in a mob.

"Give us the travelers," they say. "We're going to rape them."

(Guess where the word "sodomy" comes from.)

"Oh no, these are my guests," Lot answers." Take my daughters instead."

(Genesis 19:1-8; pp. 85-87)

This is one of the stranger incidents in the Bible. Remember I said idolatry is taking a good idea, like being healthy, and turning it into a religion? Lot takes the idea of hospitality and decides it outweighs all other responsibilities, including those to his daughters.

The city of Sodom is destroyed, but not before Lot and his wife and daughters are permitted to flee. The angels tell them not to look back at Sodom, but Lot's wife looks back and is turned into a pillar of salt.

(Genesis 19:15-26; pp. 87-89)

I pointed out earlier that unless we aggressively reject them, the values of our community gradually become our own. Furthermore, association taints us with the crimes of our society.

Lot and his wife live in a cruel and selfish place, and they share its values. God permits them to flee, but to do so they need to disown Sodom and "turn their back upon it." Lot's wife can't do that.

Under a government which imprisons any unjustly, the true place for a just man is also a prison.

Henry David Thoreau

This Section Rated R

Lot and his daughters hide in a mountain cave. They believe that the entire world has been destroyed, and that they are the last people left alive. The older daughter says to the younger, "There is no man [left] in the land to marry us. Let's get our father drunk, and sleep with him, and in that way we can have children." (Perfectly reasonable, right?) They get Lot drunk and have relations with him. Each conceives. The first names her son Moab which means "from my father." The second names her son Ben-Ammi, which means "the son of my people."

(*Genesis* 19:30-38; *pp. 89-91*)

Not Again

With Sodom destroyed, the flow of travelers dries up, and there is no one on whom Abraham can lavish his care. He travels to Gerar (near Ashkelon on the Mediterranean coast.) Again Abraham and Sarah pose as brother and sister. Again Sarah is kidnapped and taken to the king—in this case, Avimelech. God appears in a dream to Avimelech. He tells the king he is guilty of kidnapping another man's wife and warns him to release Sarah. Avimelech protests that his intentions were innocent and his hands clean. God acknowledges that Avimelech's *intentions* were innocent but says he is nevertheless guilty because of what he had done.

Because "the road to hell is paved with good intentions," we are accountable for our *actions*, and evil can't be excused by arguing that its perpetrators meant well. Stalin and Mao murdered millions in the vain hope of making a better world. Asked to justify the wholesale slaughter of the middle class, the Bolsheviks responded. "You can't make an omelet without breaking some eggs."

A Boy Named Laughter

As God promised, Abraham and Sarah have a child. They name
him Isaac, which in Hebrew means "laughter."

(Genesis 21:1-3; p. 95)

What kind of name is that for a kid?

Isaac's name expresses the joy his parents feel at the unanticipated wonder of his birth. The birth of a child is *always* a miracle, but because Abraham and Sarah are already old, the miracle of his birth is even greater. On a deeper level, Isaac's name anticipates the wonder that will constantly attend the lives of his descendants—a people involved in a continually unfolding relationship with God.

Get That Kid Out of the House

After Isaac's birth, Sarah recognizes that Ishmael is a bad influence
in their house. (The Talmud says Ishmael mocked the covenant with
God. The laughter of wonder expresses joy at the miracle of life. The
laughter of ridicule destroys all sense of sanctity.) Sarah asks Abraham
to send Ishmael away. Abraham resists Sarah's advice, but God agrees
with her and tells Abraham to do what Sarah asks.
"Listen to Sarah's voice," God says. "She is a greater prophet than you."

(Genesis 21:9-12; p. 97)

Raise 'em Right

Isn't this cruel?

It's a parent's responsibility to supervise who his children play with. As kids get older, parents and family diminish in their influence, and the influence of friends and peers grows greater. If you want your children to grow up properly, you can't be indifferent to who they play with.

IT'S Simple

This is one of many instances in the Bible where a woman's insight changes the course of Jewish history. Many people imagine that the Bible considers women less important than men, but anyone who thinks that hasn't read the Bible very carefully. Stay tuned.

A Small Request

God tells Abraham to offer Isaac as a burned sacrifice on a mountaintop. Abraham travels for three days to God's designated place (Mount Moriah in Jerusalem, where Solomon will later build the Temple.) Abraham binds Isaac with rope and lays him on a rock. Just as he is about to slaughter him, an angel of God arrives to stop him.

(Genesis 22:1-19; pp. 101-105)

This is one of the most important and troubling stories in the whole Bible. Why does God want Abraham to kill his son? Why does Abraham agree?

I Don't Buy It

◆ Everything we have is a gift. This is true not only of our possessions. The people we love and even our own lives don't belong to us. They are merely lent to us for our brief enjoyment. If you think everything is due you, your life will be filled with the bitterness of frustrated expectations. If you live without expectations, and see what comes your way as a gift, it's much easier to be happy. Observant Jews often write a line from Psalms in the inside cover of their books: "The world in all its fullness belongs to God. This book is in my temporary possession."

✦ Could anything be more precious to you than your child? Imagine the following scenario. One of the cruelest actions of the Germans in the Holocaust was to make the Jews accomplices in their own destruction. In each ghetto the Germans set up a Jewish council, called the *Judenrat*. They would tell the council, "Tomorrow a train leaves for Auschwitz at 9:00 A.M. Get a thousand children onto that train, or *your* children will be on the train. What would you do if confronted with such a choice? Is it possible murder would be a price too high to pay, even for your child's life?

✦ Or consider this situation:
I know an Israeli man who was stationed as a soldier on the Suez Canal when the Egyptians attacked in 1973. The Israeli soldiers had to choose whether to withdraw or to stay where they were. To stay meant nearly certain death, but it was a sacrifice that would offer the Israeli army time to mobilize and possibly to save the nation from destruction.

What would *you* do in that situation? What would you say if your *child* asked you what to do?

God asks Abraham to sacrifice Isaac so he'll explore what he loves most of all. He learns his love for God is even greater than his love for his son.

HELP!
I Need More Info

God stops Abraham just as he is about to kill Isaac. He tells him, "I never wanted you to kill him. I just wanted to see if you were willing to make the offer."

Adding Insult To Injury

Soon after Abraham's (non) sacrifice of Isaac, Sarah dies. Abraham
tries to buy a cave to bury Sarah in from a man named Ephron.
Ephron starts with a great show of generosity, and offers the cave to
Abraham for free. In the end, however, he demands
an exorbitant price for it.

(Genesis 23:1-20; pp. 107-109)

We saw earlier that Abraham offers little and does a lot. ("Let me bring you some bread and water," he told the three travelers, and then he brought them a feast.) Ephron is the opposite. He makes grand promises and delivers very little.

God gives Abraham ten moral tests to help him grow into the moral giant who could be a beacon for the whole world. The encounter with Ephron is the final and most difficult test.

It is easier to achieve a moment of ecstasy on some distant mountaintop than to walk with God amidst the petty frustrations of daily life. Abraham's ninth test was to offer Isaac as a sacrifice on Mount Moriah. The tenth and harder test is to come down off the mountaintop.

Some years ago, on Yom Kippur, I came home from synagogue during the afternoon break in the prayers. I tried to put one of my children to bed for a nap, and she started crying.

"Shut that kid up," my neighbor screamed over the fence.

Without a moment's hesitation, I screamed back, "If you don't like it, shut your windows." And then I had to stop and laugh at myself. It's Yom Kippur. I'm a rabbi. I'm dressed in white. And I'm screaming at my neighbor over the fence. Fast and pray all day? Piece of cake. Crying kids and nasty neighbors? *That's* a challenge.

Very Thirsty Camels

Abraham realizes he'll have no descendants unless Isaac marries,
so he decides to find his son a wife.

(Genesis 24:1-8; pp. 109-111)

Even if God promises you offspring "like the stars of the sky," it isn't going to happen if you don't do your part. There's a story about a man who prays with great intensity to win the lottery. Finally a voice booms out of heaven. "Listen, meet Me halfway. Buy a ticket."

Abraham sends his servant Eliezer with instructions to find a wife for
Isaac. Eliezer asks God's help to find the right person. He travels
through the desert to a well, and he prays that when he asks for water,
the woman God wants to be Isaac's wife will respond by offering water
not only to him but to his camels as well.

(Genesis 24:10-14; pp. 11-113)

Raise 'em Right

When the prince falls in love with Sleeping Beauty, he doesn't know anything about her goals or character—she's *sleeping*. All *she* knows about *him* is that he's charming. And then, the story says, they lived happily ever after.

People raised on fairy tales tend to believe them. But Eliezer knows marriage has to rest on something deeper than beauty. He is looking for a woman with character and goals.

I ran into a bright and successful man I know. He had recently gotten married, so I was surprised to see him looking depressed and miserable.

"Rick," I said, "what's the matter."

"I really want to have kids, but my wife doesn't want to."

"But Rick," I said, "didn't you cover that before you got married?"

"No," he said. "It never came up."

So you don't make Rick's mistake, here's a short list of what to look for in someone you might spend your life with:

✦ Find someone kind.

Being kind is very different from being nice. Nice is a synonym for polite and inoffensive. Nice people don't do gross things like insult your mother or spit on your tie. Nice is an important attribute for a waiter or doorman. But kindness is a far rarer and more important trait. Someone kind cares about *your* good and your pleasure, not only for his own. You can't make a successful marriage with someone who isn't kind.

✦ Find someone loyal.

Without loyalty marriage is impossible. Blending two people's lives into one is a frustrating challenge, and if you enter marriage leaving yourself a way out, you'll take it. (Think of the commitment of marriage as being like the commitment to your hand. It isn't absolute—if you had gangrene you might amputate your hand— but it's certainly not a commitment you'd reconsider just because "the fun had gone out of your relationship" with your hand or because you'd met someone whose hands you liked better.)

✦ Find someone whose goals in life match your own.

Buying a house or winning a job promotion isn't a life goal. A life goal is something you'd like written on your tombstone.

Without shared life goals marriage is impossible, because you can't go through life with someone if you don't know where you're going. And the goal of life can't be to get married. Marriage expands who we are, and permits us to pursue our life goals more effectively; but when depressed and aimless single people get married, they become depressed and aimless married people.

In *real* life, Sleeping Beauty and the prince don't live happily ever after. Their marriage lasts about three years.

> *Rebecca comes to the well, and Eliezer asks her for water.*
> *"Drink," she says, "and let me draw some water for your camels as*
> *well." Eliezer recognizes God has answered his prayer, and he asks*
> *Rebecca to marry Isaac. This time, they really do*
> *live happily ever after.*
>
> (Genesis 24:15-67; pp. 113-121)

CHAPTER 4

Little Children—Little Problems, Big Children—Big Problems

Isaac and Rebecca are married for many years without children.
Rebecca eventually conceives. Her pregnancy is terribly painful,
so she goes to a prophet to seek an explanation.
The prophet tells her she is pregnant with twins. The twins will grow
into nations with diametrically opposed and incompatible views of life.
Already in her womb they struggle with each other.
The first child born is Esau. He comes out ruddy and covered with
hair. Jacob is born next. He is born grasping Esau's heel
(as though seeking to overcome and supplant him).
As the boys grow older, the difference in their character becomes
more apparent. Jacob is innocent and scholarly,
while Esau is violent and passionate.
One day Abraham dies. Jacob prepares lentil stew
(a dish traditionally prepared for mourners because the roundness
of the lentils evokes the cycle of life). Esau comes in from the field.
He is tired and hungry.
"Pour some of that red stuff into me," he says, "I'm exhausted."
"Sell me your birthright," says Jacob. (The birthright is the
privileges and responsibilities of the firstborn.)
"Who cares, I'm going to die anyway," said Esau,
"What do I care about the birthright.
Take it and give me the stew."

(Genesis 25:19-34; pp. 125-129)

What does it mean?

Esau believes that since in the end we're all going to die, good and bad alike, we might as well fill our lives with intense pleasures like food, sex, and the thrill of violence. Why worry about irrelevant nonsense like spirituality or philosophical questions like the meaning of life?

Esau is the ancestor of a nation called *Edom*, which tradition identifies with Rome. (*Edom* means red, like the color of blood or of Jacob's stew.) The Romans' idea of a great evening was to watch gladiators hack each other apart, and then top it off with a drunken orgy. Our own enjoyment of blood sports like boxing stems back to Rome. More profoundly, the influence of Roman culture encourages us to dismiss religion as wishful thinking and to believe that the goal of life is to satisfy our appetites.

> *It [is] not true that there is a power in the universe, which watches over the well-being of every individual with parental care and brings all his concerns to a happy ending. Dark, unfeeling, and unloving powers determine human destiny; the system of reward and punishments, which according to religion, govern the world, seems to have no existence.*

Freud, <u>New Introductory Lectures on Psychoanalysis</u>

If so, then what is the purpose of human life?

> *What is the purpose of human life? Nobody asks what is the purpose of the lives of animals ... it is [a striving to eliminate] pain and discomfort, [and to] experience intense pleasure ... from the satisfaction of pent-up needs which have reached great intensity, and by its very nature can only be a transitory experience.*

Freud, <u>Civilization and its Discontents</u>

In other words, in the end I'm going to die anyway—so bring on the stew!

How can Jacob take such callous advantage of Esau's hunger?

Misplaced kindness can cause lots of human suffering. In the preface to his history of World War II, Winston Churchill wrote that "the theme [of this history is] how the English-speaking peoples through their unwisdom, carelessness, and good nature allowed the wicked to rearm."

Jacob recognizes that Esau's love of cruelty is incompatible with the mission of Abraham. He takes advantage of Esau's moment of weakness to prevent much greater tragedy.

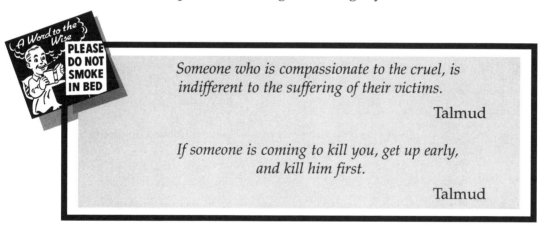

Someone who is compassionate to the cruel, is indifferent to the suffering of their victims.

Talmud

If someone is coming to kill you, get up early, and kill him first.

Talmud

Esau, I'm Feeling Peckish

Isaac isn't aware that Esau sold his birthright to Jacob. As the end of his life draws near, Isaac decides to bless his children. (Blessing someone is something like seeing their potential and encouraging them to fulfill it.) Isaac tells Esau to catch a deer and make stew. After eating, Isaac intends to bless Esau with the power and responsibility of leading Abraham's descendants. Isaac knows Esau is neither a saint nor a scholar, but he's impressed by Esau's potential and his charisma.

Esau is also very manipulative, and he knows how to speak in ways that make him appear pious. (Hitler's demand for the Sudetenland, the industrialized strip of northern Czechoslovakia, was couched in complaints that "the German nationals of the Sudetenland are being denied their legitimate rights of self-determination." Hitler the democrat!)
Rebecca sees that Esau's piety is a fraud and that he is ruled by his passions. She dresses Jacob in Esau's clothing.
She puts goat skins on his arms and hands to mimic the rough hairy feel of Esau's skin.
She makes a stew, and sends Jacob to Isaac. Isaac thinks Jacob is Esau. He eats the stew, and then he gives Jacob the blessing to lead the children of Abraham.

(Genesis 27:1-29; pp. 135-139)

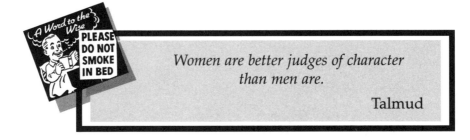

A Word to the Wise

PLEASE DO NOT SMOKE IN BED

Women are better judges of character than men are.

Talmud

Eat And Run

Esau returns, and realizes Jacob has stolen his blessing. He bursts out crying. Isaac gives Esau a blessing also, but the birthright has passed over to Jacob.
Esau decides that when Isaac dies, he will kill Jacob. Rebecca intuits Esau's plan and asks Isaac to send Jacob to Charan (Abraham's original home) to find a wife. Jacob leaves for Charan. Esau remains behind, gnashing his teeth and planning his revenge.

(Genesis 27:30-28:9; pp. 139-143)

Tell Your Therapist About This Dream

Jacob stops for the night at the place of Abraham's (non) sacrifice of Isaac, Mount Moriah. He sleeps, and dreams that angels are mounting and descending a ladder to heaven, while God stands at the ladder's top.

(Genesis 28:10-15; pp. 145-147)

Ice cream and jacuzzis are good (we aren't meant to be ascetics). But life also offers greater pleasures, like love, beauty, and awe. These are *spiritual* pleasures—moments when the physical world hints at eternity. A ladder on which the angels shuffle, intimately links the physical and spiritual worlds. And God stands at the ladder's head.

Trust Me

Jacob continues on to Charan. There he meets his cousin Rachel and decides to marry her. He tells her father, Laban that he will work for him for seven years for Rachel's hand.
The night of the marriage, Laban substitutes Rachel's older sister, Leah in Rachel's place. In the morning, Jacob is surprised. Laban justifies his deceit by saying, "We don't let the younger daughter get married before the older." Then Laban tells Jacob, he can also marry Rachel, if he works another seven years.

(Genesis 29:1-27; pp. 147-153)

Laban means "white," but Laban is anything but innocent. Though his true motives are selfish, Laban, like Esau, knows how to clothe his selfishness in pious rhetoric. In movies villains are ugly. They sneer and wear black. But it is a dangerous illusion to believe that evil is always obvious. In *real life*, villains dress elegantly and speak the Queen's English.

A Gaggle of Kids

Leah immediately conceives and in quick succession gives birth to
Reuben, Shimon, Levi, and Judah.
Rachel is initially barren. As Sarah did before her, she gives her
maidservant, Bilhah, to Jacob as a surrogate mother.
Bilhah gives birth to Dan and Naftali.
Leah gives her maidservant, Zilpah, to Jacob.
She bears Gad and Asher.
Leah conceives again and gives birth to Issachar,
Zebulun and to a daughter, Dina.
Rachel finally conceives, and bears Joseph. (Rachel later gives birth
to a final child, Benjamin, and dies in childbirth.)

(Genesis 29:31-30:24; pp. 153-157)

I Don't Buy It

Thirteen children?

A child is more special than a Rembrandt. Would you decline the chance to own a valuable masterpiece because caring for it is too much work? Or imagine you could count gold pieces from a chest, and keep them. Would you take a nap or watch television instead? Our lives are like that chest of gold. We have a brief chance to make something special of our lives, and then the opportunity is gone.

We become confused, however, between comfort and pleasure. *Comfort* is the absence of pain, like falling asleep on a warm beach. *Pleasure*—like marriage, wisdom, children, or helping people in need—is achieved only with effort and discomfort. The gold is there for the taking, but many people choose instead to take a nap or watch reruns instead.

Despite Laban's efforts to take advantage of him, Jacob becomes
wealthy. He leaves Laban's house, and heads home.
Laban wants to kill Jacob, but God protects him.

(Genesis 30:25-32:3; pp. 157-169)

Living with Laban tests Jacob's ability to maintain his integrity. Being an ethical rabbi is child's play. Being an ethical businessman is a great achievement.

I Came, Esau, I Conquered

Jacob sends a message to his brother Esau, telling him he's coming home. The messengers return to tell Jacob that Esau is coming toward him with an army of four hundred men. Believing Esau plans to kill him, Jacob divides his camp into two, so if one is destroyed the other can flee. He prays to God for help, and he sends presents to Esau to appease him.

(Genesis 32:4-24; pp. 171-175)

We've seen before that success requires practicality *and* God's help. If you're sick, pray and go to a doctor. When you go to war, pray and oil your gun. As he prepares to confront Esau, Jacob covers all his bases.

God Stuff

That night, a man comes and confronts Jacob in his tent. All night the two wrestle, but neither can defeat the other. As dawn breaks, the man reveals he is an angel.
"Let me go," he says, "for dawn has broken."
"I won't let you leave unless you bless me," says Jacob.
The angel blesses Jacob and he says to him, "From now on, your name is not 'Jacob,' but 'Israel.'"
As the sun rises, Jacob limps on, his sciatic nerve torn in the confrontation with the angel.

(Genesis 32:25-33; pp. 175-177)

What does this mean?

Jacob and Esau represent incompatible views of life. In Esau's violent, hedonistic world, there is no room for the gentle spirituality of Jacob. The angel is Esau's angel. Their nightlong struggle symbolizes that through the dark night of history, Jacob and Esau will struggle to impose their stamps upon this world. It is a battle to the death, which Jacob will survive by his wits. (*Jacob* means "crafty." It implies the perpetual underdog, exiled, wounded, but never destroyed.) In the end, however, the dawn of redemption will break, and the world-view of Jacob will emerge victorious. (*Israel* means one who has struggled and ultimately triumphed.) This story foretells that the world will ultimately renounce the violence and hedonism of Esau and turn to the values of Israel.

In the morning, Jacob and Esau meet. Esau is softened by Jacob's presents and when Jacob speaks to Esau with deference and respect, he is appeased. Esau kisses Jacob and the brothers part.

(Genesis 33:1-17; pp. 177-181)

It is one of the spiritual laws of the universe: Esau hates Jacob.

Talmud

Their confrontation ends in apparent friendship, but anti-Semitism, the hatred of Esau's descendants for the children of Israel, persists throughout history.

Jacob comes with his family to the city of Shechem. His daughter, Dina, goes into town to look around. Dina is kidnapped and raped by

the city's prince. (To make things confusing, he's also called Shechem.)
Jacob's sons suggest that if the people of Shechem will consent to be
circumcised, everyone can still live together in peace.
The townspeople agree, and they circumcise themselves. Three days
later, two of Dina's brothers, Shimon and Levi, go into the town.
They rescue Dina, and slaughter everybody else.
Jacob rebukes them for what they have done.
They answer him, "Could we let our sister to be treated like a harlot?"

(Genesis 33:18-34:31; pp. 181-185)

Jacob doesn't tell Shimon and Levi their actions were immoral. Shechem was a murderous little village, and when it was destroyed, property values surged for miles. Jacob tells them their sense of outraged justice wasn't tempered with common sense and judgment.

Shimon and Levi exemplify a character trait called *kina*, which means zealous rage at evil. Like all character traits, zeal can be used for good or for bad.

Zeal makes miracles possible. (The triumph over the Greeks celebrated by Hanukkah was led by a descendant of Levi, Judah Maccabee. *Kina* led him to begin a rebellion that soberer spirits would have dismissed as Quixotic.) But passion is also blind, and *kina* can lead to terrible misjudgment and destruction.

CHAPTER 5

Think You've Got Trouble
With Your Kids

Jacob Takes a Rest

By this point, Jacob has already lived a very eventful life. He was forced to flee home as a child to escape Esau's wrath. He spent twenty-two years in exile, raising thirteen children. He evaded Laban's efforts first to cheat and then to kill him. Then Esau tried to kill him together with all his family. His daughter was raped, and his sons wiped out a medium-sized village. He is tired and craves some peace and quiet. Just then new troubles arise. They consume most of the remainder of Jacob's life.

We distinguished earlier between *comfort* (the absence of pain) and true *pleasure*, achieved at the price of effort and frustration. We want pleasure, but because pleasure is hard work, we often choose comfort. Daydreaming is less work than thinking. Watching television is less effort than talking to your children. Sleeping is more comfortable than waking, and the perfect comfort is death. Jacob wants to retire from the effort of living. God brings him new troubles to keep him awake and grappling with the meaning of being alive.

IT's *Simple*

The Bible is mercilessly honest about people's faults and makes clear that Jacob's youngest son, Joseph, is a nightmare of a little brother. Vain and foppish, he continually runs off to tell Jacob bad things the other kids have done. Worse, he is clearly Jacob's favorite, and as a mark of favoritism, Jacob gives Joseph a splendid coat of many different colors. (Don't add this to your list of effective parenting techniques.) Then to be *really* endearing, Joseph tells his brothers a couple of his choice dreams.

"We were binding bundles of wheat in the field, and guess what happened! My bundle stood upright, and your bundles all gathered around and bowed down to mine!"
The brothers love that one. They are even fonder of the next one.
"The sun (my father) and the moon (my mother) and eleven stars (that's you) were bowing down to me!"

(Genesis 37:5-9; p. 201)

In praise of the brothers, the Bible says they are so angry with Joseph, they can't speak to him nicely. They aren't two-faced flatterers. They can't stand him, and they tell him so.

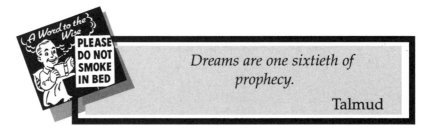

Dreams are one sixtieth of prophecy.

Talmud

One day the brothers take the sheep out to graze. Jacob sends Joseph to Shechem to find them. (Note that violent things happen repeatedly in Shechem.) The brothers see Joseph coming and do what many of us want to do to our little brothers.
"Let's kill him," they say, "and tell Dad he was eaten by a wild animal."

*Reuben persuades them not to kill Joseph. Instead, they strip him of
his colorful coat, and sell him to a caravan of merchants
bringing slaves for sale to Egypt.*

(Genesis 37:12-28; pp. 203-205)

I always wanted to murder or sell *my* little brother, but aren't
people in the Bible supposed to be better than the rest of us?
And having faults is one thing. But isn't kidnapping your
brother and selling him going a little too far?

The Bible wouldn't teach us anything if it were about
perfect people who never make mistakes (because that isn't
real life). Rather, it's about people who struggle with themselves and with each other, just like we do. Their moral greatness
isn't that they don't make mistakes. It's that instead of *accepting*
their faults, they keep trying to improve. No one in the Bible says,
"Love means never having to say you're sorry."

My teacher, Rabbi Weinberg, told me a story that *his* father told
him.

*Early every morning, the rabbi went by himself to the synagogue. His
students didn't know what he did there, and one morning they hid to find
out.*

*Entering the synagogue, the rabbi opened the ark and began to take
out the Torah scroll. Then he drew back and spoke to himself.*

*"Your students think you're wise and holy. But you know how
inflated their view of you is and how far you fall short of what you ought
to be."*

*"That's true," he answered himself. "I really need to try harder." And
again he began to remove the Torah from the ark.*

*"You made the same commitment yesterday," he remonstrated, "and
again you made all the same mistakes."*

*Back and forth the rabbi argued with himself. Then finally he said,
"Today I will be better," and he took the scroll out of the ark.*

Though jealousy warps the brothers' judgment, there is logic to their actions. Their family *had* its problems. Abraham's son, Ishmael, was such a bad influence that God told Abraham to drive him from the house. Isaac's favorite son, Esau, was a homicidal maniac. The brothers believe that Joseph too, with his egocentric vanity and readiness to damage them in their father's eyes, is fundamentally bad and a danger to them all.

The brothers dip Joseph's coat in blood and bring it to their father.
"Do you recognize your son's coat?" they ask.
"Maybe he was eaten by a lion."
Overwhelmed with grief and pain, Jacob puts on sackcloth (a rough
and scratchy shirt people wore as a sign of extreme anguish).
He mourns his son and his grief is inconsolable.

(Genesis 37:31-35; p. 207)

It Seemed Like Such a Good Idea

With Jacob's intense grief before their eyes,
the brothers regret their actions. Though not the oldest,
Judah is the de facto leader of the group, and they decide it was his
fault that they sold Joseph.
(Call it a cop out, or call it the responsibility of leadership.)
Judah moves away. He marries and has three sons, Er, Onan, and
Shelah (the names Jack, Joe, and Billy being much too common).
Er marries Tamar. Er dies and it becomes Onan's duty to marry Er's
widow. (This custom, called yibum, is a way of perpetuating the lineage
of a brother who dies childless.) Onan marries Tamar, but he refuses to
consummate the marriage, and then he also dies.

*After Onan's death, Shelah is next in line to marry Tamar, but Judah
prevents him, fearing the same fate that befell
Tamar's first two husbands.
Tamar dresses as a prostitute and waits where she knows Judah will
pass. Judah doesn't recognize her. He has relations with her and leaves
her his staff and signet ring as collateral for payment due. Tamar
conceives. Judah sees that Tamar is pregnant but doesn't realize he is
the father. He orders her put to death for adultery. Tamar sends
Judah's staff and ring to him.
"These belong to the man who is the father of my child," she says.
"Do you know who that person is?"*

(Genesis 38:1-25; pp. 209-213)

What goes around comes around.

One thing you see in the Bible a lot is measure for measure. Jacob tricked Isaac, pretending to be Esau. Leah tricked Jacob, pretending to be Rachel. Judah failed to save Jacob's son, and loses his own sons in turn. Tamar's precise words to Judah, "Do you recognize who this staff and seal belong to?" echo the brothers earlier words to Jacob, "Do you recognize your son's coat?"

We don't appreciate the harm we've done others until a similar fate befalls us. Measure for measure is God's way of helping us grow.

IT's Simple

Joseph's journey to Egypt in bondage begins a series of events leading to the slavery of Jacob's descendants, the first of many exiles for the nation of Israel. The descendants of Peretz,

God Stuff

Judah's son by Tamar, lead to King David and from King David to the Messiah and the final redemption of the Children of Israel. (We'll talk more about the Messiah later.) Even as the people start their long journey into exile, God is preparing their final redemption.

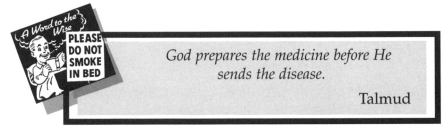

> *God prepares the medicine before He sends the disease.*
>
> Talmud

Confronted with irrefutable evidence he is the father of Tamar's child, Judah confesses, and he proclaims Tamar's innocence.

(Genesis 38:26; p. 213)

The ability to admit your mistakes is a rare but crucial trait of true leadership. When the prophet Natan accused King David of stealing another man's wife, David immediately confessed his guilt. (He didn't claim executive privilege, and have his secretary erase the tapes.)

Joseph is sold as a slave to Potiphar, a powerful noble in the court of the Egyptian King, Pharaoh. Joseph is exceptionally capable, and gradually Potiphar transfers to Joseph all the responsibilities of running his business and his household. Besides being capable, Joseph is also extremely good looking. Potiphar's wife tries to seduce Joseph. When he refuses her advances, she accuses him of trying to rape her, and Joseph is thrown into prison.

(Genesis 39:1-20; pp. 213-217)

I Had a Dream

Two of Pharaoh's servants, a butler and a baker, are in prison with
Joseph. The butler has a dream that he is pressing three grapes into
wine and handing the wine to Pharaoh. The baker has a dream that
birds are eating from three baskets he carries on his head.
The dreams seem portentous, but the butler and baker are unable to
understand their meaning. They tell the dreams to Joseph.
Joseph tells the butler that in three days he will be restored to his post.
He tells the baker that in three days Pharaoh will cut off his head.
Joseph's predictions are fulfilled. As the butler is freed,
Joseph tells him, "Remember me, and get me out of here,"
but the butler forgets him, and Joseph spends another
two years in prison.

Now Pharaoh starts dreaming. He dreams that seven fat cows
emerge from the River Nile. Seven thin cows follow them
and eat the fat cows, leaving no trace.
Pharaoh has another dream. He dreams that seven healthy ears of
grain sprout on a stalk, followed by seven thin and withered stalks. The
thin stalks consume the healthy ones, and again nothing remains.
Pharaoh is unable to decipher the meaning of his dreams. He calls
his wise men, and he demands that they interpret the dreams.
Now the butler remembers Joseph. He tells Pharaoh about the
young Israelite who correctly interpreted his dream. Joseph is rushed
from prison, bathed, shaved, and brought before Pharaoh.
"The interpretation of dreams belongs to God," says Joseph (who
seems to have learned a lot of humility in prison).
"God is sending you a message through your dreams. The seven fat
cows are seven years of plenty. The seven skinny cows are seven years
of famine. The famine will be so severe that it will leave no trace
of the plenty that came before.
"The dream about the ears of wheat has the same meaning. The
repetition of the two dreams together means that this will happen soon.

*"Now find a wise man who will gather Egypt's grain into storehouses
during the years of plenty, so when the famine comes
there will be something to eat."*

*Pharaoh is extremely impressed by this. Without further ado,
he changes Joseph's name to Zaphenath-paneah
(try spelling that for the receptionist),
and appoints him Prime Minister of Egypt.
Through the years of great plenty, Joseph gathers up grain
and stores it. Then the years of famine begin,
and people come from around the world to Egypt to buy grain.*

(Genesis 40:1-41:57; pp. 217-231)

Meanwhile, In a Small Town To the North

*The famine affects Canaan as well. Jacob and his sons have nothing
to eat. Jacob sends them to Egypt to buy grain.
He keeps home only Benjamin, who with Joseph's disappearance,
is the only son remaining
to him from his beloved wife Rachel.*

(Genesis 42:1-5; p.233)

Imagine a fly walking across a man's head as the man strolls down the aisle of a speeding train as the earth revolves on its axis and circles round the sun in a rapidly expanding universe. How fast is the fly travelling and in which direction? Joseph's brothers sold him as a slave to Egypt because they hated him. In Egypt, Joseph becomes Prime Minister so he can store up grain, so Jacob's family can find refuge from the famine, so they will eventually become enslaved there, so the stage will be set for the eventual exodus. Who controls events, and in which direction do they tend? We have freedom of choice, but our choices become part of a tapestry of whose larger texture we may only dimly be aware.

God Stuff

Joseph was sold into slavery as a young boy. It is twenty-two years
later when his brothers come to Egypt to buy grain. They don't
recognize him, but he recognizes them. He speaks to them harshly.
"You are spies!" he says. "You have come here
to spy on the land of Egypt."
"No, no," they answer. "We are twelve brothers, one of whom is
dead. (They mean Joseph.) Our youngest brother
is with our father in Canaan."
"I will not believe you unless you bring your youngest brother here
too," Joseph tells them, "and I will keep one of you here
in prison until he comes."

(Genesis 42:6-20; pp. 233-235)

We all make mistakes. Our mistakes damage us and create distance between us and the people we love.

The Bible's prescription for fixing our mistakes is called *teshuva*, which means "return"—returning back to where we were and who we were, before our mistakes sent our lives askew.

Part of *teshuva* is saying "I'm sorry," but being sorry isn't enough. The real indication we've changed is when we're put in the same position we were before and we don't act the same way.

Remember Joseph's dreams of the stars and the sheaves of wheat bowing down to him? The dreams tell Joseph how to engineer the brothers' return to the same choice they faced twenty-two years earlier when they sold him. To make the dreams come true he needs all the brothers in Egypt.

On With the Story

Joseph puts Shimon in prison. He fills the other brothers' sacks with grain and surreptitiously returns their money to their bags as well. He warns that he will sell them no more grain unless they return with their youngest brother, Benjamin. The brothers return home, unload their sacks, and are confused and disoriented when they discover that their money has been returned to them. Jacob is distraught that Shimon has been left imprisoned in Egypt. Afraid that Benjamin will disappear, as Joseph and Shimon did before him, Jacob adamantly refuses to permit him to accompany the brothers back to Egypt. The famine grows harsher. Jacob tells the brothers to return to Egypt for grain, but they remind him that they cannot return without Benjamin. Judah personally guarantees Benjamin's safe return, and with starvation the only alternative, Jacob finally relents. Benjamin and his brothers go to Egypt.

When they arrive, they are brought to Joseph's palace. Joseph dines with them and shows particular favor to Benjamin. While they eat, their bags are filled with grain, and Joseph's servant hides an expensive silver goblet in Benjamin's bag.

The brothers begin their return to Canaan. Joseph sends a messenger, who overtakes the brothers and accuses them of stealing the silver cup. They protest their innocence and declare that if the charge is true, they will become Joseph's slaves. The sacks are opened, and the cup is found in Benjamin's sack.

"You needn't all be my slaves," Joseph tells them, "just the youngest one, who stole it. The rest of you may go."

Suddenly, the brothers' passivity and indecision vanishes. With a careful blend of confrontation and deference Judah challenges Joseph. He describes what Benjamin's loss would mean to Jacob, and he begs Joseph for compassion.

Unable to control himself, Joseph bursts out, "I am Joseph.
Is my father still alive?!"
The brothers, stunned, are silent.

(Genesis 42:24-45:3; pp. 237-253)

What happened?

Envy and suspicion caused the brothers to hate Joseph. They envied him Jacob's love, and his own actions bred suspicion. After Joseph's disappearance, Benjamin is Jacob's favorite, and the cup planted in his bag offers the brothers grounds to believe he is a thief. Through his careful plot, Joseph creates the same poisonous combination of envy and suspicion that led the brothers to sell *him* twenty-two years earlier. But this time the brothers refuse to betray Benjamin.

Joseph's outburst, "Is my father still alive?" also needs explanation. Judah just appealed to Joseph to consider the pain Benjamin's enslavement would cause to Jacob. But Joseph's words are a final rebuke to his brothers.

"I see how concerned you are for our father," he tells them. "Where was that concern when you sold me?"

Joseph loads the brothers' sacks with food. He tells them to bring
Jacob and the rest of the family to take refuge from the famine in
Egypt. The brothers return to Canaan and tell Jacob that his favorite
son, missing for twenty-two years, is still alive.
And Israel (Jacob) says, "How great! My son Joseph still lives!
I shall go and see him before I die."

(Genesis 45:21-28; pp. 255-257)

Y ou may remember that after Jacob wrestled with Esau's angel, Jacob's name was changed to Israel. Sometimes the Bible calls him by one name, and sometimes it calls him by the other. When he is just a private individual, he is "Jacob." When he embodies the future nation, he is "Israel."

When he believed Joseph was dead and all hope of a nation lost with him, then he was "Jacob," an old man burdened with sadness. When he discovered Joseph was alive, his hope revived of a great nation that would personify God's presence in the world. Then he became "Israel."

As individuals we are short-lived, frail, and vulnerable. As an expression of something larger and nobler than ourselves, our lives are uplifted, sanctified, and transformed.

IT'S Simple

W hen trauma strikes, we are often overwhelmed with pain and sorrow. But sometimes, through that pain, we can discover new opportunities have been opened in our lives. As long as he believed that Joseph was dead, Jacob was crushed with sadness. When he discovered Joseph was alive, Jacob realized that God's love had never abandoned him.

A prophecy from the days of Abraham had told that the Children of Israel would go to Egypt in exile. They might have gone there in chains. They went instead drawn by the cords of Jacob's love for his son.

God Stuff

A Nation On the Move

Jacob and his family head for Egypt. On the way, God appears to Jacob in a dream. He tells Jacob that in Egypt the small tribe of his descendants will be transformed into the nation of Israel and that they will then return to possess the Land of Israel. He also reassures him, that "Joseph will place his hands on your eyes."

(Genesis 46:1-4; pp. 257-259)

W hen someone dies, we close his eyes, as though to say "This world is now hidden from you."

Though we know we must die, the terror of that awareness is softened by the assurance that our children will continue our presence in the world. They will be our eyes once the darkness of death closes around us.

IT's Simple

Jacob sends Judah ahead to make preparations for the family's arrival in Egypt.

(Genesis 46:28; p. 261)

J udah's preparation is to establish a school for the study of God's commandments to Abraham. Jacob's first priority is that his children not forget their heritage during the sojourn in Egypt. This can only be achieved through education.

HELP! I Need More Info

To further discourage his family's assimilation, Joseph wants them physically separated from the Egyptians. He settles them in Goshen, on the outskirts of the populated area of the country.

(Genesis 46:31-47:4; p. 263)

The United States has provided a haven for generations of refugees. As they assimilate into America, each new ethnic group contributes flavor to the melting pot of our polyglot culture, while shedding the ties which bound them to their homelands. But assimilation has not been kind to Jewish survival. Of the 8.1 million Jews in America today, 1.1 million practice no religion, and 2.6 million practice a religion other than Judaism. For every ten Jews who marry in America today, seven marry non-Jews. Joseph doesn't want this to happen to his family in Egypt. That's why he settles them apart.

The famine continues. Joseph sells grain to the Egyptians, acquiring their money, livestock, and land as payment. Finally, with all their other resources exhausted, the Egyptians sell themselves as serfs to buy grain. The Children of Israel meanwhile, become wealthy and prosperous in Egypt. (If you think this bodes well for the future, think again.)

(Genesis 47:13-27; pp. 265-267)

It's Time To Say Goodbye

Jacob senses his death approaching. He begs Joseph to bury his body in Canaan in the cave where Abraham, Sarah, Isaac, and Rebecca were buried. Joseph swears to fulfill his father's wishes.
Jacob tells Joseph that Joseph's sons, Ephraim and Menashe, will inherit equally with Jacob's other eleven sons. This double portion confirms Joseph's position of leadership of the family and fulfills his prophetic dreams of many years before.

(Genesis 47:28-48:6; pp. 269-271)

A Blessing On Your House, Mazel Tov, Mazel Tov

Before dying, Jacob blesses his children.
The strengths and weaknesses of the various children define the
character of each of the twelve tribes. Together, these tribes
make up the nation of Israel.
In blessing his sons, Jacob also defines the relationship
between the future tribes of Israel.
Here is some of what he tells them:

✦ *Reuben—You have the greatest potential of any the brothers, but*
you lack the stability and judgment to be a leader.

✦ *Shimon and Levi—Cursed is your anger, because it is cruel.*
Though your passion for justice is praiseworthy,
zeal often overwhelms your judgment.

(Genesis 49:1-7; pp. 275-277)

Jacob doesn't curse Shimon and Levi. He curses their anger. It's a parent's responsibility to help his children grow by correcting their mistakes. But when you rebuke them be careful to emphasize that you love them, it's just their behavior you don't like.

In proper measure, spice adds flavor. In excess, it mars the dish. Similarly, the influence of these zealous tribes is best diffused. When the Land of Israel is later divided among the tribes, Levi receives no portion. Instead, his tribe is scattered throughout the land—diffusing his influence, like pepper, throughout the nation.

✦ *Judah—You are the true leader, the one whose willingness to*
admit your mistakes ordains you for true greatness.

(Genesis 49:8-12; pp. 277-279)

Since Judah (in Hebrew, *Yehuda*) was the leader, the Children of Israel came to be known as Yehudim, or Jews.

✦ Zebulun and Issachar—Issachar is a scholar. Zebulun is a merchant. Since Zebulun's financial support permits Issachar to study, you two have a symbiotic relationship.

(Genesis 49:13-15; p. 279)

It isn't a Biblical ideal that everyone be a rabbi. Just as each limb contributes toward a complete body, each tribe and each individual contributes something unique toward the complete nation.

✦ Dan—You are a snake.

(Genesis 49:16-17; pp. 279-281)

This is a prophetic reference to Samson, a descendant of Dan. In the time of Samson, the Israelites were oppressed by a nation called the Philistines. Samson attacked them stealthily, catching them unawares, like a snake.

The blessings highlight that all character traits are neutral (neither inherently good nor bad). Intelligence, strength, beauty—all can be used for great good or for great evil.

Jacob promises his children God will send a redeemer to take them from Egypt. Then he dies. After Jacob's death, the brothers fear Joseph will revenge himself upon them.

He reassures them that though they meant to hurt him,
God turned their murderous intention to advantage.
If not for his position of power in Egypt,
the entire family might have starved
during the famine.

(Genesis 50:15-21; pp. 287-289)

We are culpable for our choices. But the measure of our culpability depends as well on the outcome of our actions. (That's why there are different penalties for murder and for attempted murder.)

Before he dies, Joseph again reassures his family.
"God will surely remember you," he tells them,
"and He will bring you up out of this land to the land that
He swore to Abraham, to Isaac, and to Jacob."
Joseph dies. The Book of Genesis ends with the seed of the
future nation of Israel planted in Egypt.

(Genesis 50:22-26; p. 289)

PART II

Exodus
The Birth Of A Nation

The second book of the Bible is called Exodus. This is the part where the Israelites leave Egypt and go into the desert.

Lots of strange and unusual things happen in this book. Sticks turn into snakes, the sea splits, and bread falls from the sky. It is one of the most important stories ever told, because through these events the Israelites, the Egyptians, and the whole world learn what it means that there's a God.

If you've ever been bored at a Passover *seder*, start here. If you want to know why "let my people go" became the rallying cry for liberation movements through history, you're also in the right place to start.

CHAPTER 6

What Have You Done For Me Lately?

Joseph and all his brothers die. A new generation arises with no memory of the patriarchs, and begins rapidly to assimilate into Egypt. There is also a new generation of Egyptians who has long forgotten Joseph's service to Egypt. The Israelites seem to be a dangerously powerful minority in Egypt. The Egyptians are fearful and jealous of them, and so they enslave them.

(Exodus 1:1-14; pp. 293-295)

Through the centuries of Jewish exile, tolerance and assimilation have alternated with persecution and oppression.

In the late nineteenth century, the most prominent financier of Prussia's unification of Germany was a Jewish banker named Gerson Blechroder. Blechroder's children converted to Christianity and intermarried. His grandchildren were deported to Auschwitz.

In Hebrew, the word for "man" is *zachar*. The word for "memory" is *zecher*. Memory doesn't just tell us where we've left our keys. It tells us who we are. We are the sum of the experiences that have formed us, and when the Israelites forget their ancestors, they forget the meaning of their own identity.

The Egyptians force the Hebrews to build massive storehouses. To break their spirit, they impose meaningless labor on them (like piling and repiling mounds of rocks).

Pharaoh orders the Hebrew midwives to kill all infant boys.
But the midwives fear God. They do not do as the king of Egypt tells
them, "and they cause the boys to live."

(Exodus 1:14-20; p.295)

There is a popular impression that Jews in the Holocaust went passively to slaughter, but this is a slanderous misimpression. It takes courage to fight, but when there is no option to fight (and the Jews of Eastern Europe had none), it takes greater courage to nurture hope against every encouragement to despair.

Rabbi Israel Spira, a Holocaust survivor, tells of the morning a group of children were taken from their parents to slaughter.

Suddenly, just next to us, I heard the voice of a woman.
"Jews, have mercy upon me, and give me a knife."
In front of me stood a woman, pale as a sheet. Only her eyes were burning. I looked around, and since I saw no Germans in sight, I said to her, "Don't kill yourself. Why rush to get to the World of Truth? We will get there sooner or later. What difference can one day make?"
"Dog, what did you say to the woman?"
A tall young German appeared from nowhere, swinging his truncheon above my head.
"The woman asked for a knife. I explained to her that we Jews are not permitted to take our lives. Our lives are entrusted to the hands of God."
The German handed the woman a knife and stepped back to watch her kill herself.
The woman lay a bundle of rags upon the ground, and unwrapped it. Amidst the rags, on a snow-white pillow was a newborn baby, asleep.
The woman recited a blessing, "Blessed art Thou, O Lord our God, King of the universe, who has sanctified us by thy commandments and has commanded us to perform the circumcision."
And then she circumcised the baby.

She straightened her back, looked up to heaven, and said, "God of the Universe, you have given me a healthy child. I am returning to you a wholesome, kosher Jew."

She walked over to the German, gave him back his bloodstained knife, and handed him her baby on his snow-white pillow.

That's courage. That was the heroism of the midwives.

Pharaoh tells the Egyptians to throw the Hebrew babies into the Nile. Rather than bring children into the world to see them murdered, men separate from their wives. Then in an act of hope and faith, a man named Amram reunites with his wife, Yocheved. She conceives and bears a son. They hide him as long as they can. When they can hide him no longer, they place him in a basket at the edge of the river. Pharaoh's daughter comes to the river to bathe and finds the basket. Moved to compassion by the baby's tears, she takes him into the palace and raises him as her son. She names him Moses.

Then one day when he is grown up, Moses goes out to his brothers and sees their oppression. He sees an Egyptian murdering a Hebrew. He looks around, and when he sees there is no man there, he kills the Egyptian and buries his body in the sand.

(Exodus 1:22-2:12; pp. 297-299)

The repeated description of the Hebrews as "Moses' brothers" emphasizes his kinship with them. Raised in the splendor of Pharaoh's palace, it was an act of great moral courage for Moses to identify with a rabble of oppressed slaves.

Until very recently, a Jewish name was a bar to professional advancement in this country. Think of the temptation to succeed by passing as a gentile. Imagine the calculation that turned Ralph Lipschitz into Ralph Lauren.

IT'S *Simple*

The next day, Moses again goes out. This time he sees two Hebrews fighting. He intervenes, and the toughest one taunts him. "Do you plan to kill me like you killed the Egyptian?"

(Exodus 2:13-14; p. 299)

When the Soviet Union invaded Afghanistan, the head of the trauma medical center at UCLA was Dr. Bob Simon.

Simon wanted to know who was caring for the refugees in Afghanistan. He wrote to Medicine Sans Frontiers (an organization that provides medical care in war-torn countries) and a variety of United Nations agencies, but no one was doing anything because the Russians were shooting any doctors they found in the country. Simon said to himself, "I guess it's up to me to do something."

He sold his house and moved to Pakistan. In Pakistan he trained Afghani refugees as medics, teaching them how to remove bullets, splint broken bones, and treat the most common diseases. Then he sent his medics back across the border to Afghanistan to provide the only medical care available in the country until the Soviet Union pulled out.

Though the Bible says Moses saw "no man" when he killed the Egyptian, from the words of the two Hebrews it's clear someone must have been there. But Moses saw there was "no man" prepared to take responsibility and to act. He saw it was up to him.

Moses flees Egypt to avoid Pharaoh's vengeance, and he goes to Midian. He is sitting by a well when the daughters of Jethro, the priest of Midian, arrive to water their flocks. Local shepherds try to drive them away, but Moses intervenes and protects them. Moses goes to live with Jethro and marries his daughter, Tzippora.
Pharaoh dies, and is replaced by a new Pharaoh, who increases the Hebrews' oppression. Crushed by their torment, the Hebrews cry out to God, and God hears their cry.

(Exodus 2:15-25; pp. 299-301)

A man falls over a cliff. At the last moment, he grabs hold of a branch and hangs swaying above the precipice.

He calls out "God save me!"

A voice from heaven answers, "I will save you. Just let go of the branch."

The man thinks about this for a minute, and then he calls out again, "Is anyone else up there who can save me?"

Why didn't the Hebrews cry out for God's help before? Perhaps they couldn't cry out until they knew they had no options for helping themselves.

There's Something You Don't See Everyday

Moses is shepherding Jethro's flock in the desert. He sees a bush burning. Watching closely, he notices that though the bush keeps burning, the flames don't consume it.

Then God calls out, "Moses, Moses."

"Here I am." Moses answers.

(Exodus 3:1-4; p. 301)

M oses' answer, in Hebrew *hineni*, is the same answer as Abraham's when God told him to sacrifice Isaac. *Hineni* means I am ready to do whatever you will ask me.

A burning bush that isn't consumed is hardly a megaphone. We're talking *subtle*.

The need for meaning in our lives (for that is the voice by which God calls out to us) is subtle. It is frequently drowned out by the demands of work, by our fears and appetites, and by the hustle and bustle of our lives. A man less sensitive than Moses might have ignored the burning bush and gone right on watching television.

> **T**he burning bush was a metaphor for the Hebrews in Egypt. Though the flames of oppression danced about them, the Children of Israel were not consumed.

God tells Moses, "Remove your shoes.
You are standing on holy ground."

(Exodus 3:5; p. 301)

Life's greatest pleasures are pleasures of the soul, not the body. (Sex is good, but love is better.) Preoccupation with the body's needs interferes with true pleasure.

The mystical tradition explains God's words metaphorically. The body clothes the soul as shoes clothe the feet. By telling Moses to remove his shoes, God invites Moses to shed the limitations that his physical body impose upon his vision and to rise to a higher plane of perception.

God tells Moses to go to Egypt and free the Israelites. Moses objects
to this plan: "Me? Who am I to free the Israelites?"
God tells him: "You're making a mistake. You're not taking the
Children of Israel out of Egypt. I'm taking them out of Egypt.
You're just my emissary."

(Exodus 3:7-12; pp. 303-305)

If God asked you to tell Saddam Hussein to leave Israel alone, you might believe you'd been confused with someone else—like Superman, for instance.

But God explains to Moses that his choices are merely the opening through which God can make miracles happen.

A man trapped by a flood calls out to God to save him. A jeep comes by and the driver offers to carry the man to safety, but he declines.

"No," he says, "God will save me."

The waters rise and he continues to pray.

A boat comes, but once again the man declines help.

"No," he says, "God will save me."

The waters continue to rise.

A helicopter flies over and drops a rope to pull the man to safety.

"No," he says, "God will save me."

Then he drowns.

He goes to heaven.

"Why didn't you save me?" he asks God.

"I sent you a jeep," God says, "and a boat, and a helicopter!"

> *Then Moses asks, "The Israelites will ask me what God's name is.*
> *What shall I answer them?"*
> *God answers, "My name is 'I will be what I will be."*

(Exodus 3:13-14; p. 305)

Moses tells God the Israelites won't understand how an abstraction like God can free them from Pharaoh's whips and chains.

God answers that the physical world does not limit Him. Rather, His unfettered will is the underlying reality of our world. (We discussed this concept in Part I when we explained that God is the sustainer of our world. The purpose of the plagues is to demonstrate that this is true.)

> *Moses says the Hebrews won't believe God sent him.*
> *God tells him to throw his stick on the ground, and it turns into a*
> *snake. Then He tells Moses to put his hand into his shirt, and when he*
> *pulls it out, it is leprous. God tells Moses that if the Hebrews doubt*
> *him, these signs will dispel their doubts.*

(Exodus 4:1-9; pp. 307-309)

> hese signs also warn Moses he is slandering the Israelites. A leader needs to believe in the greatness of the people that he's going to lead.

Moses objects that he stutters.
God tells him, "I will be with your mouth and tell you what to say."

(Exodus 4:10-12; p. 309)

Hollywood has frozen the image of Charlton Heston in our minds as Moses—tall, bronzed, and powerful. But the Bible emphasizes that the Hebrews' freedom is due neither to their courage nor to Moses' charisma. God set them free.

The Passover Haggadah doesn't even mention Moses. Moses is a cipher—the tool God uses to set His people free.

Moses says to God, "Can't you just send someone else?"
At this point God gets angry with Moses.

(Exodus 4:13-14; pp. 309-311)

The holiday of Purim revolves around a Jewish woman named Esther, who became queen of Persia. When the king decided to kill the Jews, Esther's uncle, Mordechai, begged her to intercede, but Esther was afraid and vacillated.

Mordechai told her, "If you don't act now when you have the chance, the Jews will still be saved, but you and all your father's household will be lost. It was for this very opportunity that you were given the privilege of power."

While Moses asks reasonable questions, God answers patiently. But when his anxiety and inaction merely prolong the people's suffering, God gets angry.

The opportunity to do something meaningful is precious and fleeting. To squander the opportunity is a serious moral failing.

A Guy With An Attitude

Moses returns to Egypt, and with his brother Aaron, he tells
Pharaoh that God demands the Children of Israel be set free.
Pharaoh tells them, "I've never heard of God. I have no intention of
freeing the Hebrews. And if they have leisure to think about freedom,
it means they're not working hard enough."
Then he doubles the Hebrews' work quota.

(Exodus 5:1-14; pp. 313-315)

Our own lives are often informed by Pharaoh's malicious prescription that being busy will shear us of thought.
The television goes on as soon as we wake up in the morning. In the car, the radio goes on. All day we're busy at work. As we drive home, the radio plays. The evening is filled with more television, and then we go to bed—no moment of the day is spared for peaceful contemplation that might permit us to consider who we are and what our lives are really about.

The Children of Israel blame Moses for the increase of their burdens.
Moses is also upset and disappointed. He says to God, "I did just what
you told me to do, but things got worse, not better!"
God rebukes Moses. He reminds him that though the patriarchs,
Abraham, Isaac, and Jacob never saw the fulfillment of God's promises,
they still maintained their faith and trust.

(Exodus 5:20-6:8; pp. 319-321)

People sometimes imagine that religion is a cosmic guarantee against crabgrass, but this is a shallow view. While pain, sorrow, and disappointment rock everyone's life, God gives us the strength and hope to persevere. Faith gives us the confidence that our suffering is not in vain.

*Someone [without faith] is like a tree whose branches
are many but whose roots are few.
The wind comes and uproots it, and turns it upside
down ... and he shall be like an isolated tree in an arid
land and shall not see when good comes.
He shall dwell on parched soil in the wilderness,
on a salted and uninhabited land.*

*But someone [with faith] is like a tree whose
branches are few but whose roots are numerous.
Even if all the winds in the world were to come
and blow against it, they could not budge it from its
place ... and he shall be like a tree planted by waters,
spreading its roots toward the stream.
He shall not notice the heat's arrival,
and his leaves shall be fresh.
In the year of drought he shall not worry,
nor shall he cease from bearing fruit.*

Jeremiah 17:6-8

Eat Your Heart Out

*God tells Moses to throw his stick on the ground before Pharaoh.
He does so, and the stick turns into a snake.
Pharaoh summons his magicians and advisors. They too throw sticks
on the ground and turn them into snakes.
Then when everyone is laughing in ridicule at Moses, his snake
turns back into a stick and swallows all the other snakes.
Everyone stops laughing. Then Pharaoh hardens his heart.*

(Exodus 7:8-13; pp. 325-327)

Pharaoh got it. He recognizes he is dealing with a power greater than he can understand. But he can't accept the consequences of admitting he is wrong, so he hardens his heart.

In the middle of an argument, we are sometimes shocked and discomfited to discover we are wrong. The natural instinct at that point is to change the topic or argue louder. That instinct is the Pharaoh in each of us— the egotism that believes we could never be wrong. If your desire to be right is stronger than your desire for insight, you'll never learn anything.

The Ten Buzz Kills

God tells Moses to meet Pharaoh at the Nile River,
early in the morning when Pharaoh goes to bathe.
(Pharaoh claimed to be a god, immune from normal bodily needs
so Moses caught him with his pants down.)
Aaron strikes the river with his staff, and it turns to blood.
Pharaoh summons his magicians,
who also turn water into blood. (This has always seemed to me a truly
dumb thing to do. Who needs more blood?
If the magicians are so smart why don't they turn
the blood back into water?)
The next plague is frogs that swarm from the river and infest the
land of Egypt. Not to be outdone—you guessed it—the magicians
make more frogs. This time Pharaoh finds it unbearable and agrees to
let the people go if Moses will make the frogs go away.
But as soon as the frogs are gone, Pharaoh hardens his heart again
and refuses to let the Israelites go.

(Exodus 7:14-8:11; pp. 327-331)

Why does Pharaoh agree to let the people go, and then change his mind?

We all have had moments when we recognize the need to change—watch our weight, stop yelling at our children, or use our time more productively—but attacks of conscience are rarely fatal. The next day, the sun is shining. Routine reasserts itself, and we go right on living the way we did before.

This **AFFECTS** *YOU*

At God's command, Aaron strikes the dust with his staff and turns it into lice. The magicians are unable to replicate this plague, and they tell Pharaoh, "This is the finger of God."
But Pharaoh won't listen, and so it goes on, through another seven plagues:
wild animals
pestilence
boils
hail
locusts
darkness
death of the first born

(Exodus 8:12-10:29; pp. 331-345)

HELP!
I Need More Info

The darkness is so thick and impenetrable that the Egyptians are unable to move. For a Hebrew in the same room, however, there is plenty of light.

I Don't Buy It

After the sixth plague—boils—the Bible says that, "God hardened Pharaoh's heart," but this seems grossly unfair! How can God warn Pharaoh to obey and then harden his heart so he can't listen?

God doesn't want to coerce Pharaoh to let the Israelites go. He wants Pharaoh to admit he is wrong. But the plagues are so overwhelming and frightening, Pharaoh almost gives in against his will. So God hardens Pharaoh's heart to help him do what he wants to do, which is to go on saying no.

There is another, more unsettling, explanation of God's hardening of Pharaoh's heart. Having been pig-headed for so long, Pharaoh loses the ability to change. If you recognize the truth and refuse to act on what you know, you dig yourself into a rut that gets deeper and deeper.

While Moses brings most of the plagues, Aaron turns the Nile into blood and the dust into lice. Moses is indebted to the river, where his life was saved as an infant, and to the dust that hid the body of the Egyptian who he killed. Because they benefited Moses, it is inappropriate he should strike them with his rod.

Of course, you don't really have to be grateful to dust, but the Bible wants us to understand how important gratitude is. Any benefit we've ever received is a debt forever.

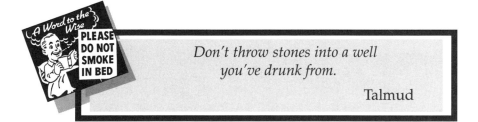

Don't throw stones into a well you've drunk from.

Talmud

What is the point of all these plagues?

Until Abraham, the world believed there were many gods—separate powers with influence over each of the different forces of nature.

The plagues demonstrate that there is one God and that all aspects of the world are dependent on God's will. Because God's will sustains the world, there is no way to hide from His power. If you align yourself with God, there are no limits.

Time To Go

God tells Moses that after one final plague, the Israelites will leave Egypt. Then He gives Moses instructions to prepare for the exodus:
✦ *Sanctify the month.*
✦ *Separate a lamb for the Passover sacrifice.*
✦ *Eat matzah and bitter herbs.*

(Exodus 11:1-12:8; pp. 347-351)

✦ *Sanctify the month*

God tells Moses to set up a calendar for the Hebrews, making the current month the first month of the year.

Why Does a Calendar Matter?

An accountant needs a calendar to know when to pay taxes. A farmer needs a calendar to know when to plant and harvest. A Jew needs a calendar to know when the holidays are coming.

Holidays don't commemorate dead incidents of the past. They are opportunities to grow *now*. Passover, for example, is not merely about the passage to freedom of long ago. It is an opportunity for us to become free—of fear, ego, or whatever else may enslave us. The calendar keeps track of the year's spiritual opportunities.

All the things you didn't want to know about biblical time keeping, but were afraid someone might tell you anyway:

There are two different ways of measuring a year: A solar year is 365 days long—the length of time it takes the earth to make one revolution around the sun. A lunar year is twelve lunar months—twelve cycles of the moon. The lunar year measures 354 days.

The Bible uses the solar calendar to mark time for the nations of the world. The lunar calendar is used to mark time for the Israelites. The mystical tradition, the Kabbalah, suggests that just as the moon reflects the sun's light, so the Children of Israel are meant to reflect the light of God.

IT'S Simple

✦ *Separate a lamb for the Passover sacrifice*

Each Hebrew family designates a lamb, and sets it aside. On the evening of the Israelites' deliverance from slavery in Israel, they slaughter the lamb, roast and eat it. The lamb's blood is placed on the doorposts of their houses as a sign Israelites live in those homes.

HELP! I Need More Info

The name Passover comes from this offering. When God kills the Egyptian firstborn, He passes over the homes whose doors are smeared with blood.

Can't God Tell Who's Who Without a Sign?

When oppressed people become free, they are frequently just as brutal as their erstwhile oppressors. It turns out that it is not oppression they objected to. They'd just prefer to be on the other end of the whip.

Society's values implicate us unless we explicitly repudiate them. As a condition of their freedom, God demands that the Hebrews withdraw from Egypt and reject its values. (The same idea helps explain why Noah had to shut himself up in an ark to escape the flood and why Lot and his wife were told to walk away from Sodom without looking back.) The Hebrews mark their separation from Egypt by going into their homes, shutting their doors, and marking them with the blood of their sacrifice—the sign of their devotion to God.

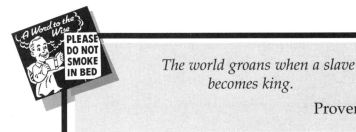

The world groans when a slave becomes king.

Proverbs

✦ Eat Matzah

Though many know the Israelites eat *matzah* because their speedy departure leaves no time for the dough to rise, careful reading of the Bible shows God told them to eat *matzah* in Egypt before their departure. What's the connection between freedom and eating crackers?

Leaven represents ego. (The difference between a *matzah* and a slice of Wonderbread is just a lot of hot air.) Self-concern is the most insidious and oppressive enslavement there is. Freedom comes from dedication to something greater than our own needs—the will of God.

The people finish their preparations. Each family eats the lamb, and smears its blood upon their doors. At midnight God kills all the firstborn of Egypt. With an anguished cry, the Egyptians drive the Hebrews out. After two hundred and ten years of slavery, the Children of Israel are free.

(Exodus 12:29-41; pp. 357-359)

We draw on our experiences for the insight and confidence we need to confront new challenges. Passover has become part of the world's memory. It is a continual reminder that though we feel trapped and helpless, we can be freed and our lives transformed in an instant.

CHAPTER 7

Let's Get The Heck Out Of Here

*The moment the Israelites leave Egypt, Pharaoh regrets their release
and chases them. (Some people never, but never, learn.)*
*The Hebrews come to the Red Sea shores. Suddenly behind them
they see the pursuing Egyptians. Panicking, they turn on Moses and
scream at him in fury, "Did you bring us out here to die in the desert?
Weren't there enough graves for us in Egypt?" (The Egyptians aren't
the only ones who never learn. No matter how many times God comes
through for the Children of Israel, they seem to flip out the next time
things get rough. Change is hard.)*
*Moses starts to pray for help, but God tells him, "Moses, this isn't
the time for prayer. Do something."*
Moses stretches his staff over the sea, and the sea splits.

(Exodus 13:17-14:22; pp. 367-373)

The sea doesn't actually split until the first man, Nachshon,
walks into the water. When the level of the water reaches
his nose, *then* the sea splits.

We can accomplish miracles with God's help, but we have
to take the initiative, and through the opening created by our
choices, God will change the world.

God Stuff

A Word to the Wise

PLEASE
DO NOT
SMOKE
IN BED

*Make an opening [for God], like the eye
of a needle, and He will open it up for
you like the broad gates of the Temple.*

Talmud

The Hebrews cross on dry land in the midst of the sea.
The Egyptians follow. When the Hebrews reach the other side, Moses
raises his staff, and the sea returns to its place.
The Egyptians drown, and the Hebrews are saved. In exultation, they
burst into a song of joy for their deliverance,
and for the destruction of their enemies.

(Exodus 14:23-15:21; pp. 373-381)

Isn't it a little mean-spirited to sing when people drown?

Unpunished, evil robs us of our faith that life is just and meaningful. The Hebrews sing because when they see the Egyptians drown they recognize that God cares about justice.

> Simon Wiesenthal spent his life tracking down German war criminals. I asked him whether he wasn't tempted to kill them rather than bring them to trial.
>
> *He answered, "This guy kills a thousand people and I kill him. What's the equivalence in that? I want to bring him to trial so the whole world can repudiate his evil."*
>
> ◆
>
> *Those who love God hate evil.*
>
> Psalms

Unfortunately, if it's far enough away, evil is pretty tolerable. As Mel Brooks said, "Tragedy is if I cut my finger; comedy is if you fall into an open sewer and die."

Hey Moses, What Have You Done For Us Lately?

*The Israelites travel into the desert. For three days they find no
water. When they do find water, it is too bitter to drink, and the people
complain against Moses. God shows Moses a branch to throw into the
spring, and the water became sweet.*
God tells them, "If you listen to God, everything will be sweet."
The people journey on, and they find no food.
Again they complain to Moses:
*"If only we had died in the land of Egypt! You took us out into the
desert to kill us from hunger."*
*God tells Moses He will rain bread out of the heaven
for the people to eat. The bread is called manna.*

(Exodus 15:22-16:36; pp. 381-389)

It seems implausible and fantastic that food should fall from the
sky, but we take for granted far more impossible things, like the
development of a human being from two cells invisible to the
naked eye. What we've never seen, we think impossible; what
we're accustomed to, we take for granted. This is called being
closed-minded.

The *manna* has many special qualities:

◆ Every day just enough falls for that one day. None can be
saved for the following day.
◆ The location where the *manna* falls is a daily report card
on each person's relationship with God. If yesterday you
walked with God, today the *manna* falls at your doorstep. If
yesterday you were selfish and self-indulgent, today's *manna*
falls far away, and you have to trouble yourself to go look for it.
◆ The *manna* is absorbed directly into your body, leaving no
waste product.
◆ It doesn't fall on the Sabbath.
◆ It tastes like whatever you want it to.

Delivered fresh daily

God wants the people to appreciate that they can rely on him.

If your daughter wanted to wrap up and save her leftover dinner "in case tomorrow you decide not to feed me," you'd know you had a serious parenting problem to address.

Do the Israelites integrate the *manna's* lesson that God can be counted on? Don't count on it.

God Stuff

Daily Report Card

Like all important relationships, a relationship with God has rewards, but also makes demands. The Israelites feel oppressed by God's daily feedback on their actions.

The Bible refers to God as "our father in heaven," but a friend of mine points out that people would prefer a *grandfather* in heaven. Grandparents are all love with no demands. Parents, like God, offer love, but they also have expectations.

The Israelites travel on, and again they have no water.
This time they attack Moses so viciously he says to God, "I think
they're going to kill me!"
God tells Moses: "Take your staff and stand before a rock. Hit the
rock, and it will give water for the people to drink."

(Exodus 17:1-7; pp. 389-391)

Like the Israelites in the desert, each of us is surrounded with the evidence of God's love and care. We're alive. We can think, speak, move, breathe, see, hear. But we're still filled with bitterness for things we don't have.

Someone once complained to me that they felt depressed.

This AFFECTS *YOU*

"If you had all your same problems," I asked, "but additionally you were blind, would it cheer you up to recover your sight?"

"Of course."

"Guess what," I said, "you've got sight."

"Yeah, but I've always had sight, and so does everyone else."

That's the secret of misery. Take everything you have for granted, and carefully focus on what you *don't* have, and you'll always be miserable.

Anyone with children knows the untutored state of man is dissatisfaction.

You take your kids to Disneyland. They go on ninety-seven rides and spend the day eating ice cream. You give them pizza for dinner and read them seventeen stories before bed. Then they ask for a cookie, and when you say no, they burst into tears.

Junket From Hell

The Israelites are attacked by the nation of Amalek.
Amalek slaughters those who straggle behind the main camp of the
Israelites. They castrate their victims and fling their genitals at heaven,
as if to say, "Here's what we think of your covenant with God."

(Exodus 17:8-16; pp. 391-393)

Amalek is a grandson of Jacob's brother, Esau.

Jews have been hated for many reasons. They've been hated for their poverty and for their wealth; for being different and for trying to assimilate; for being Communists and for being capitalists. Amalek hates them for a reason that's simpler and more profound—because the Israelites represent God's presence in the world.

The raging passions, fears, and violence of our animal nature struggle continually against the impositions of conscience. Amalek embodies this primitive and barbaric drive, and the Bible says "never forget" there are forces in the world that are hostile to all that is good and moral.

The First Convert

> *Moses' father-in-law, Jethro, hears of all that has happened since Moses' return to Egypt. After Amalek's attacks, Jethro goes to join the Children of Israel.*
>
> (Exodus 18:1-5; p. 395)

Switzerland sat out World War II as a "neutral country." But in a war against Nazism, how is neutrality possible? Jethro joins the Israelites after Amalek's attack because he recognizes that in the epic struggle between good and evil neutrality is impossible. He has to take sides.

Jethro's conversion directly precedes the revelation of the Ten Commandments. (Similarly, on Shavuot, the holiday commemorating that revelation, we read about Ruth—a Moabite convert and the great-grandmother of King David.)

There is no obligation for gentiles to convert to Judaism. But the truth revealed at Mount Sinai is not parochial. There is one God for the entire world, Jew and gentile alike.

Who Needs Business School?

> *Jethro sees Moses sitting all day judging the people. Jethro says to him, "You can't possibly do this all yourself. You're going to wear out. You should set up a system of judges."*
> *So Moses sets up a system of lower and superior courts.*

Jethro suggests that Moses seek judges who are God-fearing (concerned with doing what's just, even if it isn't popular) and wealthy (to protect them against the temptation of bribery). Further, Jethro counsels, "find men who know there are more important things in life than making money."

(Exodus 18:13-23; pp. 397-399)

Money doesn't buy happiness, and billionaires aren't necessarily happier than the rest of us.

Forbes Magazine

God tells Moses to gather the Israelites at the base of Mount Sinai so He can speak to them.

(Exodus 19:10-14; pp. 403-405)

While the world's religions portray revelation as the private experience of an individual prophet, Judaism is unique in its claim that the entire nation heard God speak. One reason people believe the Bible is true is that it's hard to fabricate a claim of this nature and magnitude if it isn't true.

The difference between having your *own* revelation and relying on someone else's account is nicely illustrated by the following story:

The rabbi of a small town dies, and the town elders debate which of the rabbi's children should replace him.

One of the rabbi's children comes and says to the elders, "My father appeared to me in a dream last night, and said I should be the new rabbi."

"If your father wanted you to be the rabbi," the elders reply, "he should have appeared to us in a dream last night!"

Here Come the Big Ten, So Listen Up

I. I *am the* Lord, *your* God

(Exodus 20:2; p. 407)

S ounds like a statement. What's the commandment?

The commandment is to know there is a God. That's different from *believing* there's a God, or having *faith*.

✦ Faith is based on *no* evidence or even goes *against* the evidence. Expecting candidates to keep their campaign promises is an example of (blind) faith.

✦ Belief is based on partial evidence, evidence not adequate for complete certainty. Thinking a corporation's past success indicates continued future success is an example of belief.

✦ Knowledge is based on fully adequate and compelling evidence. We know the sun will rise tomorrow in the East.

The Bible commands us to base our commitment to God on solid evidence. Otherwise, our religious beliefs are an accident of where we were born and of how we grew up.

If we were born in Iran, we're probably Moslems. If we were born in Sicily, we're probably Catholics. If we were born in Jerusalem, we're probably Orthodox Jews. And if were born in the United States, we probably believe there is no such thing as absolute truth.

IT'S
Simple

How can you know that there's a God?

✦ The world is *orderly*. Think of the complexity of the eye or of the brain. The patriarch Abraham decided the world's beauty, complexity, and order were evidence of God's design. Scientific understanding of the world doesn't weaken this conviction. On the contrary, the more you understand how the world works, the more awe-inspiring it becomes.

✦ The world is *wonderful*, which means it provokes wonder, and *marvelous*, which means it is something to be marveled at. Somehow, all of us sense that being alive is touched with transcendent mystery. If we're just hunks of meat and blood scrambling around for food on the third rock from the sun, it ain't that special.

✦ We need *meaning*. It isn't enough to get up every day, eat, sleep, propagate, and wait for death. We need a sense of transcendent purpose. So basic is this need that if we lose our sense of purpose, it's hard to go on living. If there isn't a God, life has no purpose. It's just waiting for the reruns.

Order, complexity, beauty, meaning, awe—these are subtle clues, but many people, including me, think if you follow them, they'll lead you straight to God.

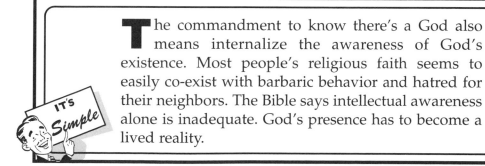

The commandment to know there's a God also means internalize the awareness of God's existence. Most people's religious faith seems to easily co-exist with barbaric behavior and hatred for their neighbors. The Bible says intellectual awareness alone is inadequate. God's presence has to become a lived reality.

This is the first of the Ten Commandments, because if there is no God, then there's no morality at all.

As a little boy, I was playing chess one day with a little girl who lived next door. Toward the end of the game she moved her castle around a corner and took my king.

"Hey!" I said. "That piece doesn't go that way!"

"Yes it does," she said.

Some like vanilla. Some like strawberry. Some enjoy kindness. Others enjoy torture. If there is no God, there are no rules. And each person's taste is as good as another's.

Why "I am the Lord *your* God"? Didn't you say there is one God for the whole world?

There is one God for the whole world. But He has a special relationship with the nation that accepts his commandments. The Talmud makes this point with a story.

God offers the Romans the Ten Commandments. They say, "Maybe. But before we accept, tell us what's in them."

God tells them, "Don't murder."

"Forget it! This Sunday we have tickets to watch Christians get fed to lions in the Coliseum!"

Then God goes to another group and offers them the commandments.

"First tell us what they are," they say.

"Don't steal."

"Forget it! Our business could never survive it."

God offers the commandments to the Israelites.

The Israelites say, "We'll take the commandments, whatever they are."

Because they are willing to follow wherever God will lead and to do whatever He will ask, the Israelites gain a special and intimate relationship with God.

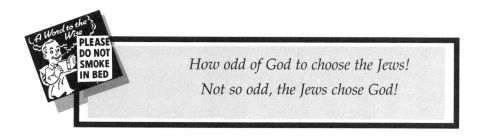

How odd of God to choose the Jews!
Not so odd, the Jews chose God!

II. *You shall have no other gods before me*

(Exodus 20:3; p. 409)

This commandment prohibits us from worshipping idols. But who could be foolish enough to pray to a statue?

In fact, adherents of idolatry didn't believe their statues were gods. They made statues to represent values to which they attached preeminent importance.

Though we no longer direct our devotion to statues, health, wealth, strength, beauty, and intelligence still remain common objects of idolatrous worship.

The most common idolatry is egotism. Nearly everyone believes that life revolves around himself.

The Bible also prohibits making images of God.

God does not exist in space or time. He is awesome and infinite beyond all imagining. If you made an image of God, you wind up thinking God is a lot like us.

In the movie Annie Hall, Woody Allen is dating a woman who's a reporter. He accompanies her to the airport to cover the arrival of an Indian guru.

"Oh," the woman gushes, "he's so wonderful. He's god."

"If you look over there," Woody says, "god is coming out of the bathroom."

The camera pans to show a fat little kid with his robe stuck in the door of the men's room.

III. Do not take God's name in vain.

(Exodus 20:7; p. 409)

This isn't a prohibition against cursing. It is a prohibition against making a false oath, or against violating an oath that you have already made.

What Is An Oath?

When Lady Macbeth tries to incite her husband to an evening of murder and mayhem, she tells him, "Screw your courage to the sticking point, and we'll not fail."

When you want to screw your commitment to the sticking point, you make an oath. You might make an oath, for example, if you're going on a diet for the eightieth time and feared your staying power might flag. You might make an oath if you want to demonstrate to someone else the absolute reliability of your words. (That's why we swear in court that what we say is true.)

If you perjure yourself, you destroy your credibility with others. But the most grievous casualty of broken oaths is your credibility with yourself. If you can't be confident you'll carry through on your own commitments, you destroy your ability to grow and change.

View whatever you say as an oath.

Talmud

In other words, say what you mean,
and mean what you say.

IV. Remember the Sabbath day and keep it holy.

*Six days you shall work, and the seventh day
is a day of Sabbath for God.*

(Exodus 20:8-9; p. 411)

We work to make a living. But work can also be much more. Part of the dignity of being human is the chance to fix and to sanctify the world. Through work, we realize our own potential.

But whether we work to meet our basic needs or whether we work to uplift the world, the Sabbath is a day to enjoy life exactly as it is. For one day a week we stop trying to get more and take pleasure in what we have.

Kindling a fire is prohibited on the Sabbath. Greek mythology viewed fire as a tool of the gods. Prometheus stole fire from the gods and gave it to man. In punishment, he was chained to a rock for eternity while an eagle ate his liver. (Bummer!)

God is more generous. He wants us to participate in creating the world. That's why the Bible says "six days work." But He wants one day set aside to figure out what we're working for.

The White Rabbit in <u>Alice in Wonderland</u> was always running late, but had no time to figure out where he was going. The week is filled with going, moving, doing, buying, fixing. The Sabbath is a time to take a leisurely stroll, to talk with friends and family, to read the book you never had the time for, or even just to think.

You've got to be careful if you don't know where you're going, 'cause you might not get there.

Yogi Berra

It is our duty ... to perfect the world under God's sovereignty.

Aleynu, an ancient Jewish prayer

V. *Honor your father and your mother.*

(Exodus 20:12; p. 411)

66 Honor your parents" doesn't mean let them tell you whom to marry. And if your parents are cruel and vindictive, you don't have to submit to their abuse.

We honor our parents by behaving as though we owe them an immense debt. We are indebted to them for the gift of being alive.

When you're dating, watch carefully how your date talks about his parents. His parents fed, clothed, and educated him. If that hasn't won his gratitude and loyalty, watch out! You won't get any either.

Because parents are central to our own identities, it's impossible to hate them and feel good about yourself.

Even more profound, your relationship with your parents establishes the model for your relationship with God. If you don't trust your parents, it's hard to trust God. If you're grateful to your parents, it's easier to learn gratitude to your parents' creator.

VI. *Don't murder.*

(Exodus 20:13; p. 411)

The last time I was in a hotel, the Bible in the drawer said "don't kill." But really, the Bible prohibits murder not killing. Murder means taking the lives of innocent people. There are, unfortunately, times that we need to kill.

Jews, Christians, and Moslems read the Bible but emerge with dramatically different religions. The uniqueness of the Jewish reading of the Bible derives from the "oral law," known as the Talmud. The Talmud explains the Bible's meaning. Without it, the Bible cannot be properly understood.

The following story illustrates this point:

A prospective convert came to Shammai, one of the great Jewish scholars and leaders at the time of the Romans.

"Convert me," he said, "on condition that I accept only the written and not the oral law."

Shammai responded as he felt the man's impudence deserved and threw him out.

The man then went to Hillel, an equally great contemporary of Shammai but famous for his calm and gentle manner.

"Convert me," he said, "on condition that I accept only the written and not the oral law."

Hillel agreed. Then he told him, "Since you accept the written law, it is essential that you learn to read," and he began to teach him the Hebrew alphabet.

When the man returned the second day, Hillel reversed the letters.

"Wait," the man said. "Yesterday you told me this was an *aleph*. Today you tell me it's a *beis*?"

"Just as you rely on me to teach you how to read," said Hillel, "rely on me to teach you the content of the law as well."

Hillel's point was that the very meaning of words is a matter of oral tradition. (If you doubt this, take a look at the Oxford English Dictionary and see how examples of usage are provided to clarify the meaning of words.)

In fact, none of the Bible's commandments could be carried out without the Talmud's explanation of how to do so. Consider the following:

◆ The Bible says, "Write these words on the doorposts of your houses and your gates."

All the words? Literally?

The Talmud explains this is the commandment of *mezuzah*. It tells us what goes in the *mezuzah* and where it should be placed.

✦ The Bible says, "Uncover your covering."
Your drapes? The messy pile on the dining room table?
The Talmud explains this is the commandment of circumcision. It tells us what circumcision is and how it is performed.

VII. *You shall not commit adultery.*

(Exodus 20:13; p. 411)

People imagine this commandment reads "Don't get caught committing adultery in the middle of a pres-idential campaign without a really clever explanation."
Without trust, you can't have love. You can't make a marriage. You can't raise children. You can't have a world.

If a man's wife can't trust him, why should I?

H. Ross Perot

VIII. *You shall not steal.*

(Exodus 20:13; p. 411)

You violate this commandment if you rob a 7-Eleven. But it's also stealing if you place a personal phone call on your employer's dime or submit a false claim to your insurance company. It's even stealing if you borrow things without permission!

I once asked my students if they would falsify information on a home loan application.

"Sure," they said.

"Do you think there's any ethical issue there?" I asked.

"What's the ethical issue?" they wondered.

"Lying," I suggested.

"But everyone does it!"

Watch out! "Everyone does it" is the most common rationalization for unethical behavior. It is estimated that if people paid their taxes honestly, the amount collected would erase the national debt.

God created Man honest, but he found many rationalizations for himself.

Talmud

IX. *You shall not bear false witness.*

(Exodus 20:13; pp. 411-413)

In the most limited sense, this is a prohibition against testifying falsely in court. But generations of commentators have explained that this commandment also includes the prohibition of *loshan hora*—"evil tongue."

Under U.S. law, you're not guilty of libel if you tell the truth. Unless there is a practical need, the Bible prohibits derogatory speech about other people even if it's true. (If you are asked to provide a job reference, that would be an example of practical need—you can tell the truth, even if it isn't pretty.)

Casual slander of other people fills our lives and conversations. (Imagine newspapers and magazines without gossip?)

We damage people by speaking ill of them, but the greatest victim of slander is the speaker. If you habitually focus on other people's faults and failings, it fills your life with poison.

Two men were walking together on the road when they passed the carcass of a dog.

"How terrible that dead dog smells," one of them said.

"Yes," said the other, "but it has lovely white teeth."

Why fill your conversation with criticism and complaints? Look for the good, and speak of that instead. You'll be happier.

X. *You shall not covet your neighbor's house/wife/ox* (Lexus).

(Exodus 20:14; p. 413)

A friend of mine many years ago went on a cruise with Harry and Leona Helmsley. Though he is very wealthy, my friend returned from his cruise green with envy of the Helmsleys' even greater wealth.

If you enjoy what you have, you'll be happy. If you envy what other people have, you'll always be miserable.

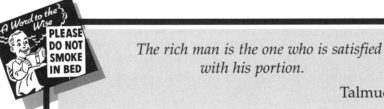

The rich man is the one who is satisfied with his portion.

Talmud

CHAPTER 8

Let's Get Technical

While it's great to commune with God in prayer, the more meaningful test of character is how we live our lives—in business, in marriage, or in war. (At the end of <u>The Godfather</u>, Al Pacino baptizes his nephew in church, while his hitmen murder his rivals in a variety of gruesome ways.)

Because the proof of real goodness is in the doing, the Bible doesn't stop with lofty spiritual and ethical prescriptions. It also mandates laws for a just and orderly society. These laws have become the basis of civil and criminal justice for the entire Western World. Here are some examples:

✦ *The Bible differentiates between premeditated murder and manslaughter.*

(Exodus 21:12; p. 421)

The penalties mandated by the Bible serve as punishment and deterrent. But their deeper purpose is to communicate the gravity with which God views the crime.

Murder, for example, is punishable by death. But in practice, the death penalty is almost never imposed.

The criminal justice system cannot establish standards of behavior. It can only support standards of behavior that society already believes are appropriate.

Because the ethical justification for Prohibition was never accepted, outlawing alcohol accomplished little.

Billions of dollars are currently spent trying to stop the flow of illegal drugs into this country, and yet the price of "crack cocaine" on the street keeps dropping.

It isn't true that "you can't legislate morality." All laws legislate morality. But it is true that you can't accomplish anything by legislating issues of disputed morality.

♦ *The Bible says that causing personal injuries is a crime, and stipulates the method to calculate fair compensation. The penalty for damages is, "An eye for an eye and a tooth for a tooth."*

(Exodus 21:22-25; p. 423)

An "eye for an eye" means compensation must be proportional to the crime and aim to "the make the victim whole." While Biblical law provides for "compensatory damages," it does not provide for "punitive damages."

In calculating damages, five factors are taken into consideration:
1. Pain and suffering
2. Loss of income
3. Medical costs
4. Emotional suffering and embarrassment
5. Impaired capacity to make a living—(e.g., I used to be in currency arbitrage, and now all I can do is polish shoes.)

♦ *If you fail to exercise proper supervision you are responsible for damage caused by your property. The Bible breaks this general category into three areas: Ox, pit and fire.*

(Exodus 21:28-36; pp. 423-425 and 22:4-5; p. 427)

1. Ox

"Ox" doesn't just mean oxen. It means any damage caused by your animals, be they goats, guinea pigs, parakeets, or cats. If Fido goes next door and chews up the neighbor's rug, you're going to have to pay. Tie him up.

2. Pit

A "pit" is any stationary obstacle left in the public thoroughfare. If you leave your skateboard on the sidewalk and a woman trips on it and breaks her leg, don't try arguing that she should have watched her step.

3. Fire

L et's say you're barbecuing in your backyard, but the wind spreads the flames and your neighbor's garage burns down. Unless the wind's strength was completely unforeseeable, you're responsible. If you put your Aztec war shield on the roof, and the wind blows it through your neighbor's window, you may think it's an "act of God," but you'll still have to pay.

♦ *It is permissible to kill in self-defense.*
(*Exodus* 22:1-2; *p. 427*)

I f someone breaks into your house, you don't have to ask whether he's selling insurance, or get involved in a long conversation about the sanctity of property. You can assume your life is threatened and kill him (unless of course you're such a good shot that you can incapacitate him with a shot in the leg).

♦ *The Bible establishes the responsibility and liability of bailees.*
(*Exodus* 22:6-14; *pp. 427-429*)

A bailee is a guardian or watchman. When you accept responsibility for someone's property, you also accept liability. If something happens to that property while it's in your care, you're responsible. The Bible identifies three different levels of responsibility, depending on how the benefits and costs of the baileeship are divided:

1. **An unpaid guardian**—Johnny is going swimming, and as he heads down to the lake he says, "Keep an eye on my wallet, will you?" You're not getting anything out of this. You're doing Johnny a favor. If you leave his wallet on the sand and go off to get some ice cream, you'll be obligated to pay if the wallet disappears. If you use reasonable care and, nevertheless, the wallet is stolen, you're off the hook.

2. **A paid guardian or a renter**—Johnny says to you, "Look here's a dollar, keep an eye on my wallet," or you say, "Johnny, here's a dollar, I'm going to rent your bicycle." In both these cases there is a mutual benefit. In the first case, Johnny gets his wallet watched, and you make some money. In the second case, you get the use of Johnny's bicycle, and he gets the money. Since you are receiving a benefit as well as giving one, your responsibility is greater. You are liable not only for gross negligence but for loss and theft under normal circumstances as well.

3. **A borrower**—You say, "Johnny, you're not riding your bicycle. Let me use it." Since you're getting all the benefit and Johnny's getting none, you have the highest degree of liability. You're liable in all cases, unless the object breaks in the course of normal use.

◆ *Give Tzedaka*

(Though I've included this among the other commandments
of social justice, the Biblical source is actually in
Deuteronomy 15:8; p. 1017)

Tzedaka refers to using your money to make the world a better place.

There are eight levels of righteousness in giving to others:

1. Give someone a loan or job to enable him to support himself.

2. Give money outright, but do so anonymously and in such a way that neither the donor nor the recipient knows the other. This way, the giver isn't doing it for the honor and recognition of giving, and the recipient isn't embarrassed.

3. Give in a way that the donor knows the recipient, but the recipient doesn't know the donor.

4. Give in a way that the recipient knows the donor, but the donor doesn't know the recipient.

5. Give directly to someone before you're asked.

6. Give directly to someone when you're asked.

7. Give a small amount, but do so graciously.

8. Give, but give resentfully.

The word "charity" comes from the Latin caritas, which means "love." *Tzedaka* means "righteousness." It's right to help someone, even if you don't care about him. If you give, you *will* care.

Israel sent an emergency medical team to Rwanda during the cholera epidemic there in the late 1990's. A friend of mine, Doctor Rick Hodes, went with them. People were dying by the tens of thousands, but despite the horror and suffering, Rick did his work with professional detachment. He worked particularly hard to save the life of a young child brought to him for care, and when despite all his efforts the child died, Rick thought he couldn't go on. But why did that one death move him more than the innumerable deaths he had already witnessed? Because he gave to that child, the child became precious to him.

Every time a poor man walks up to us on the street, we experience a moment of self-definition. If we turn away, we callous ourselves. But if we give to him, he becomes precious to us.

People sometimes say they can't believe in God because the world is so full of suffering. But I have found that people who say that are rarely involved in stopping the world's suffering. And the people who are involved in healing the world's suffering rarely talk like that. When your life revolves around yourself, the world is sterile and unfriendly. When your life revolves around giving to others, you feel how wonderful it is to be alive.

God Stuff

Bart Stern, a Holocaust survivor, told me of the time a man in Auschwitz was robbed of his daily ration of bread. Because of the starved and emaciated state of concentration camp inmates, this was tantamount to a sentence of death. Bart gave the man some of his own bread.

He told me, "The many thousands of dollars I've given to *tzedaka* since the war are nothing compared to that one piece of bread."

Bart had nothing to spare, but he nevertheless found the ability to give. Perhaps because of that, he was one of the gentlest and happiest men I ever knew. Auschwitz didn't make him bitter. It made him better.

✦ *Don't taunt or oppress a stranger, for you were strangers in*
the land of Egypt … Don't cause pain
to widows or orphans.

(Exodus 22:20-23; p. 431)

It is a natural inclination to pick on the weak, and those who
have been weak and picked on are *most* likely to revenge themselves by picking on others. The Bible warns us to exercise special
care for those incapable of caring for themselves.

✦ *Don't oppress debtors.*

(Exodus 22:24-26; pp. 431-433)

If you lend money you are entitled to repayment. You aren't
entitled to make the debtor's life miserable.

✦ *Don't curse a leader.*

(Exodus 22:27; p. 433)

Corrupt government is bad, but anarchy is worse. So
though government is not immune to criticism, be
careful not to undermine the authority on which stable
society rests.

IT'S
Simple

✦ *Don't follow the majority to do evil.*

(Exodus 23:2; p. 433)

In a classic psychology experiment, a subject is brought into a room. With him are several other people who are confederates of the experimenter (though the experiment's true subject doesn't know this).

Several lines are projected onto a screen, and the group is asked to identify which line is the shortest. The experimenter's confederates go first and intentionally identify one of the longer lines as shortest. Then the real subject is asked his opinion, and he frequently *also* identifies the longer line as shorter.

✦ *Return lost objects.*

(Exodus 23:4; p. 433)

If you see Jack's wallet slip out of his pocket, you can't wait until he turns the corner and then pick the wallet up and keep it. You have to give it back. If you see a wallet on the ground and don't know who lost it, you have to try to find the owner.

The obligation to return lost objects also includes the obligation to protect your neighbor's property from harm.

> ✦ *Don't refrain from helping someone whom you hate.*
>
> (Exodus 23:5; p. 435)
>
> **L**oving others is the ideal, but sometimes we meet someone we just can't stand. Find a way to help him, and you'll come to love him.

✦ *Don't favor the poor when sitting in judgment.*
(*Exodus* 23:6; *p.* 435)

When one party to a lawsuit was rich and the other poor, Jewish courts required both to dress in identical clothes. Then the judge wasn't swayed by the positive impression of the rich man's elegant dress or tempted to overlook justice because of compassion for the poor man's poverty.

We can't judge other human beings. Only God can properly weigh the circumstances that qualify a man's true culpability. Our responsibility is much more limited—it is to judge *actions.* Confronted with a defendant from a desperately poor and disadvantaged background, for example, a judge might say,

"Life has been unfair to you. You were hungry and deprived. Your parents were drug addicts. Your brother is a crack dealer. I have no reason to believe that in your position I would have done better. But the commandment don't steal still applies to you, and you have stolen."

Part of the challenge of child raising is recognizing it's impossible to judge our children. One child finds it easy to do schoolwork for hours. Another struggles to stay focused for fifteen minutes. Which should get a better grade for "effort?"

Until you stop judging your children, you can't help them.

Raise 'em Right

✦ *Don't accept a bribe because a bribe blinds the eyes of the wise.*

(Exodus 23:8; p. 435)

The Bible doesn't say a bribe will lead you to intentionally justify the guilty. It says when you've been bribed, you're blind—incapable of distinguishing between right and wrong.

That's why it's impossible to see clearly the people we love (or hate). Our feelings bribe us and rob us of objectivity.

✦ *Six years shall you sow your land and gather in its produce. And in the seventh year, you shall leave it untended and unharvested, and the poor of your people shall eat, and the animals of the field shall eat what is left; so shall you do to your vineyard and your olive grove.*

(Exodus 23:10; p. 435)

During the sabbatical year the poor have permission to forage where they please. This makes clear that the land belongs to no one. It is merely lent to us by God.

But the sabbatical year also reminds us that we don't belong to the land.

Successful people commonly dedicate most of their time to work. But this leaves little time or energy for other parts of life.

Ask someone, "Are you living to work, or working to live?"

"What do you think I am," he says, "a donkey? I'm working to live!"

"OK. You're working to live. What are you living for?"

Silence.

"Why not take some time from working, and figure out what you're living for?"

"I'd love to, but I don't have time!"

The sabbatical year gives us time to figure out what we're living for.

We're lost, but we're making good time!

Yogi Berra

The Biblical mandate is the origin of the academic sabbatical.

In Leviticus the Bible complements the commandment of the Sabbatical year with an injunction to observe the Jubilee year.

Count seven cycles of Sabbatical years, seven years seven times …[then] sound a shofar [on Yom Kippur] throughout the land …proclaim freedom throughout the land.

(Leviticus 25:8-9; pp. 697-699)

The Bible's command to "proclaim freedom throughout the land" is engraved on the Liberty Bell.

In the Sabbatical year, private debts are cancelled. In the Jubilee year, slaves are set free. Together these laws guarantee no man permanently subjugates another.

If you will say: "What will we eat in the seventh year? Behold, we will not sow and not gather in our crops! " I will ordain My blessing for you in the sixth year and it will yield a crop sufficient for the three-year period. You will sow in the eighth year, but you will eat from the old crop until the ninth year, until the arrival of its crop.

(Exodus 25:20-22: p. 701)

The words are a little confusing. They speak of the time when the Jubilee follows the Sabbatical year. It works out like this:

Year 49—no planting or harvesting (Sabbatical year)

Year 50—no planting or harvesting (Jubilee year)

Year 51—plant, but no harvest until year's end. Nearly three years without food! What to eat? Not to fear! God will make a miracle, and the harvest of the 48th year will last for three years. This is one reason people believe the Bible must have been written by God. Only God can promise a miracle.

✦ *Go to Jerusalem three times a year.*
(Exodus 23:14-19; p. 437)

Because it was the spiritual center of the nation, all Israelites were obliged to go to Jerusalem at Passover, Shavuot , and at Succot. (We'll talk about the holidays of Shavuot and Succot later.) Three times in a year the nation renewed its sense of unity in shared pursuit of a relationship with God.

The next time you plan a vacation, don't go somewhere comfortable for the body. Instead, go somewhere renewing for the soul! Where else? Go to Jerusalem!

When Moses finished communicating God's commands to the people, they answered with one voice, "Whatever God wants from us, we'll do!
(Exodus 24:7; p. 441)

CHAPTER 9

The Train Was Late

After receiving the Ten Commandments, Moses ascends Mount Sinai
and stays there for forty days. Uncertain when Moses will return and
fearful he has died, the Israelites feel lost and leaderless.
They make an idol of a golden calf. Then they become drunk
and have an orgy.

(Exodus 24:15-18; p. 443 and 32:1-6; pp. 493-495)

The music is just one part of a rock concert's appeal. The crowd is drunk or high; it's dark, and the noise is overwhelming. In that disorienting atmosphere of clamor and passion, we are briefly freed from our own fragile individuality and swept up in the power of the crowd. That sense of release is what the Israelites sought in their worship of the calf.

God tells Moses what the Israelites have done.
Then God says,"Now don't try to stop me,
because I'm going to destroy the whole nation."
Moses responds, "Why should You be so angry at Your people,
whom You took out of Egypt, with great power and a strong hand?
Why should Egypt say, 'He took them out to kill them in the
mountains and to annihilate them from the face of the earth?'
Remember Abraham, Isaac, and Israel ... to whom you swore,
and You told them, 'I shall increase your offspring, like the stars of
heaven, and this entire land of which I spoke, I shall give to your
offspring and it shall be their heritage forever.'"
God agrees not to destroy the people.

(Exodus 32:7-14; pp. 495-497)

Moses' argument has two parts:

1. If the Israelites don't reach the Promised Land, it will seem to demonstrate that God is weak or that His promises are unreliable. (Until the establishment of Israel in 1948, Christian theology viewed Jewish exile and suffering as evidence that God had repudiated the covenant with Abraham.)

2. Though the Israelites have made a serious mistake, it's an aberration and not reflective of who they truly are. Despite their lapse, they are still the children of Abraham, Isaac, and Jacob. (It's like meeting someone who seems to be a real schlemiel and then discovering he's Bill Gates' son. You'd probably take a second look to see if there were more to him than you had previously noticed.)

> *Moses comes down from the mountain.*
> *He gathers the descendants of Levi, and they kill*
> *everyone who was seen worshiping the calf.*
> *Then Moses grinds the calf into powder, sprinkles it in water*
> *and makes the Israelites drink it.*
> *All the people who worshiped*
> *the calf in secret now die as well.*

(Exodus 32:15-29; pp. 497-501)

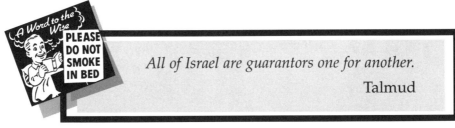

All of Israel are guarantors one for another.

Talmud

Though not everyone worshiped the calf, they are all culpable for permitting it to happen. (Think of someone drilling a hole in a boat while his fellow travelers look on indifferently.)

Moses seeks God's forgiveness for the nation's crime. Though God
agreed not to destroy the nation, He is still angry.
Now Moses wants to restore the intimate love that existed between God
and the people before they worshiped the calf.
God forgives them on Yom Kippur.

(Exodus 32:30-33:17; pp. 501-505)

Back in Genesis I told a story about the time I provoked a fight with my father and walked out of the house. I drove back to school, threw away the gold watch he'd given me, and returned his letters unopened.

Three months later, when I calmed down, I knocked on his door early one morning.

"I'm so glad you've come home," he said. "The distance between us has been terribly painful to me."

He didn't recriminate, tell me I was a louse, or demand blood in repentance. He was just happy I was home.

We all make mistakes. God just wants us to come home.

By the Way, Who Are You?

After winning God's forgiveness for the people, Moses asks God,
"Show me your glory" (which sort of means "Give me a clearer
understanding of who you are.")
God tells him, "You cannot see My face, but you can see My back"
(which sort of means "You can't understand what I am,
but I'll show you what I'm not.")
God puts Moses in the cleft of a rock.
Then God proclaims: "God, God, compassionate and gracious,
slow to anger, and abundant in kindness and truth;
preserver of kindness for thousands of generations,
forgiver of iniquity, willful sin, and error,

and who cleanses but does not cleanse completely,
recalling the iniquity of parents upon children and grandchildren,
to the third and fourth generations."

(Exodus 33:20-34:7; pp. 507-509)

Huh? Here's a rough translation: "I have placed you in a world in which you must struggle continually with confusion, with evil in the world around you, and within yourself. But though you don't always recognize it, I have made this world for your benefit. I love you more than your parents love you and more than you can ever love your own children."

> **"**Recalling the iniquity of parents upon children and grandchildren" does not mean God punishes us for our parents' crimes. It means repeating your parents' failings is a bigger mistake than making your own. If your father was an alcoholic and his drunkenness destroyed the family, then if *you* drink, you're a bigger fool than he.

Moses comes down from the mountain and his face
shines with rays of light.

(Exodus 34:29; p. 515)

The word for "rays" in Hebrew is *keren*, which is also the word for "horn." Because of poor translation of this Biblical verse, Michelangelo's statue of Moses receiving the tablets of law depicts him with horns. To this day, it is not uncommon for people from places without Jews to believe that Jews have horns. (We only wear them on weekends.)

Part III

Leviticus
Feed And Care For Your Soul

The third book of the Bible is Leviticus. This book doesn't have a story line like the first two books. Rather, God tells Moses to elevate the nation's spiritual life and tells him how to do it. The tribe particularly designated for this task is Levi, which is why the book is called "Leviticus."

If you want to know if there's a soul or if life has meaning, start here. If you want to know what the Bible has to say about holiness, you're also in the right place to start.

CHAPTER 10

Little House On The Prairie

God tells Moses to build a tabernacle, a portable temple in the desert, to be the heart of the Jewish people's national and spiritual life. God's instructions for construction of the Tabernacle begin in Exodus and are continued in detail in Leviticus.
(Exodus 25:8-9; pp. 445-447)

Who cares about this? Unless you're making an Indiana Jones movie, what possible relevance could this have today?

Life needs meaning. Without meaning, even the most comfortable life has no pleasure.

In his textbook, *Existential Psychotherapy*, the psychiatrist Irv Yalom quotes the following suicide note:

"Imagine a happy group of morons who are engaged in work. They are carrying bricks in an open field. As soon as they have stacked all the bricks at one end of the field, they proceed to transport them to the opposite end. This continues without stop, and every day of every year they are busy doing the same thing. One day, one of the morons stops long enough to ask himself what he is doing. He wonders what purpose there is in carrying the bricks. And from that instant on he is not quite as content with his occupation as he had been before.

I am the moron who wonders why he is carrying the bricks."

How do we give our life meaning? Meaning comes from a relationship with God.

In a relationship with God our actions suddenly acquire a larger context. Our choices have significance. The sense of our own being becomes enriched with permanence.

God is everywhere, but by building a Tabernacle, the Israelites create a tangible sense that God is present in their lives. The Tabernacle is a vehicle for their relationship with God.

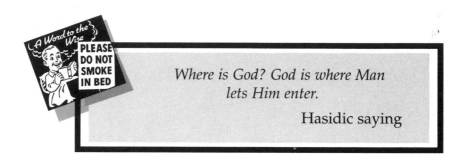

Where is God? God is where Man lets Him enter.

Hasidic saying

I sn't all this talk about God just wishful thinking designed to make us feel secure?

There is certainly good reason to hope God exists. If there is a God, we're not alone, and our lives have meaning. But just because we wish for something doesn't mean it *isn't* true.

There is also a part of us that hopes God *doesn't* exist— because then we're free to live as we please, without responsibility or fear of consequences.

Intellectual honesty demands that we weigh carefully how conflicting desires may affect our judgment.

The Tabernacle presents three paths to a relationship with God:
Kindness, wisdom, and holiness.

✦ Kindness

In the Tabernacle, the shulchan, a twelve-shelved table, symbolizes
kindness. (There are twelve shelves for the twelve tribes.)
Each shelf holds a loaf of bread, representing
the material wealth of the nation.

(Exodus 25:23-30; pp. 449-451)

L ike intellect, wealth is morally neutral. You can do great good with money. You can also do great harm. (Anyone who thinks money is an unmitigated blessing hasn't watched the debauched children of rich parents destroy their lives.)

Until it's used properly, wealth isn't an achievement. It's just an opportunity and the world is filled with wasted opportunity. The Bible doesn't preach asceticism. But exaggerated indulgence in luxury is a waste of the opportunity money offers. Wealth's real potential is the opportunity to give. Through giving to other people, we emulate God.

There is a wonderful Yiddish story called Even Higher. Roughly paraphrased, it goes like this:

A traveler comes to a small town in eastern Poland the week before Rosh Hashanah, the Day of Judgment.

The people of the town come out to greet him.

"We know why you've come," they say. "You've come to see our holy rabbi."

"The people of every town think their rabbi is holy."

"But ours is truly holy. The week before Rosh Hashanah, when the special penitential prayers are said, our rabbi goes up to heaven."

The traveler says nothing, but he decides to debunk the story of the rabbi's trips to heaven. Late that afternoon, he creeps into the rabbi's house and hides beneath his bed. At dawn, everyone gets up for synagogue, but the rabbi stays in bed. Finally, when the house is empty, the rabbi also gets up. He dons a rough peasant's smock. He binds a rope around his waist, picks up an axe and leaves the house.

From a distance, the traveler follows the rabbi deep into the forest. There the rabbi chops down a tree and cuts it into logs. He binds the logs with rope and heads back for the village. He comes to the poorest hovel and knocks on the door.

"Who is it?"

"It's me," says the rabbi, "Vasily, the woodcutter. I have wood to sell."

"I have no money to buy wood."

"I will give it to you on credit."

"I will never be able to pay you. I am too sick to work."

"Trust your God. He will give you the money."

"How can I kindle the fire? I am old and feeble."

"I will light the fire for you," the rabbi says.

The rabbi enters the shack, where an old woman lies huddled beneath a bundle of rags. He kneels and builds a fire, and as he lights it, he says the penitential prayers beneath his breath.

The traveler decides to stay in the town. He too becomes a follower of the rabbi. In future years, when the townspeople say, "Our rabbi goes to heaven during the penitential prayers," the former traveler smiles.

"No," he says, "the rabbi goes even higher."

I dropped my glasses, faintly scratching one lens. Though the scratch is barely perceptible, every time I wear my glasses, I notice the slight distortion. Imagine the soul as a fine lens scratched by every act of cruelty or burnished by every act of kindness. Though the impact of each individual choice is imperceptible, a lifetime of self-absorption gradually blinds us to the beauty of living. A lifetime of giving fills our lives with light.

✦ Wisdom

The second path to a relationship with God is wisdom.
Wisdom is symbolized in the Tabernacle by a seven-branched candelabra, the menorah.

(Exodus 25:31-40; pp. 451-453)

The menorah is an acknowledgment that God gave us the mind to look for truth—true understanding of the physical universe and true understanding of the meaning and purpose of our lives.

People imagine that science and religion are antagonists. But the more we know of science, the more awesome the world appears. Like all matter, a human being is merely atoms bound together by electrical attraction. Yet somehow this coherence of inert particles is alive. It is an "I," that can think and choose and feel. Science takes nothing away from life's wonder. It deepens it.

The most important knowledge is wisdom.

Science explores the composition of the stars and how to reach them. Wisdom asks how to apply this knowledge to improve our lives. Without wisdom, the mind can be used as easily for evil as for good.

Most of the Waffen SS held college degrees. Martin Heidegger was one of the pre-eminent philosophers of the twentieth century. He was also a Nazi. In a 1933 "Appeal to German Students," he said,

"Let not axioms or ideas be the rules of your Being. The Fuhrer himself and alone is the present and future German reality and its law."

The Tabernacle menorah had seven branches, while the one we light on Hannukah has eight. This is because when the Maccabees recaptured Jerusalem from the Greeks and rededicated the Temple, the Menorah burnt for eight days. But that's another story.

✦ Holiness

The third path to a relationship with God is holiness,
symbolized in the Tabernacle by the altar.
People sometimes imagine that holiness consists of wearing white and
speaking in a soft monotone. But holiness really means consecrating
the life of the body—making love, walking, talking,
and eating—with something in mind larger than oneself.

(Exodus 27:1-8; pp. 459-461)

The relationship between the body and the soul is like the relationship between a horse and a rider. The horse is the body, a fountain of energy and passion. Like the rider, the soul provides discipline and direction. In synchrony horse and rider have grace, speed, and power. Or imagine a ballerina, who soars effortlessly across the stage. Her grace comes through discipline, and through endless hours of practice.

Holiness is the sublimation of our power, appetites and drives to the higher purpose of the soul. And if through fear, laziness or confusion we fail to take advantage of life's opportunities, we leave our own lives unfulfilled. We leave blemished that nuance of life, which only we are capable of perfecting.

Franz Kafka tells the following parable:

A man from the country begs for admittance to the palace. A doorkeeper in front of one of the innumerable doors greets him and announces that he may not be admitted at the moment. When the man attempts to peer through the entrance, the doorkeeper warns him:

"Try to get in without my permission. But note that I am powerful. From hall to hall, keepers stand at every door, one more powerful than the other, and the sight of the third doorkeeper is already more than even I can stand."

The supplicant decides that he had better wait until he gets permission to enter. He waits for days, for weeks, for years. He waits outside that door for his entire life. He ages; his vision dims; and as he lies dying, he poses one last question to the doorkeeper, a question he had never asked before:

"Everyone strives to attain admission to the palace. How does it come about then that in all these years no one has come seeking admittance but me?"

The doorkeeper bellows in the man's ear (for his hearing, too, is fading):

"No one but you could gain admission through this door, since this door was intended for you. I am now going to shut it."

Because life is a precious asset held in trust, suicide is prohibited. As the Talmud explains it, "Your life doesn't belong to you. It is merely lent you to use appropriately."

Men In White

Aaron's descendants are assigned to serve as priests in the
Tabernacle. The priests are called Cohanim. *Their job is to serve as an*
exemplar of how people live with constant awareness of God.
The Children of Israel as a whole are called on to be a Nation of
Priests. The Cohanim are the template.

(Exodus 28:1; p. 465)

The privileges and responsibilities of priesthood were originally intended for the firstborn of the entire nation. But when
the firstborn failed to stop the Israelites from worshipping the
golden calf, the priesthood was given to Aaron's descendants
instead.

Git Yer Cotton Pickin Hands Off Those Grapes

Anything consecrated for the Temple becomes holy.
Taking Temple property is a special case of theft called
meila.

Imagine visiting Versailles, the one-time palace of the kings of
France. You look at the furniture, the gardens, the paintings
on the walls, and the books on the shelves. As you walk
through the halls, you try to understand the lives of the
people who once lived there.

The world is God's palace. Everything in the world
helps us understand God—from the stars whose light will
never reach us to the barnacles clustered on the belly of a ship.

But imagine that on your visit to Versailles, you slip a piece of
silver in your pocket, chip some gilt from a chair, and spill wine on
the carpet. That's *meila.*

The Almighty wants us to enjoy the world as we try to
understand Him. *Meila* means looting the world to indulge our
gluttony.

Don't Try This At Beth Shalom

God tells the Israelites the laws of sacrifices. Sacrifices are primarily brought in atonement for serious crimes.

(Leviticus 1:1-8:36; pp. 545-587)

Animal sacrifices?

Imagine you make a very serious mistake that leaves you feeling alienated and distant from God. You take a cow—a large, expensive, warm-blooded animal with soulful brown eyes and you bring it to the Temple. You rest your hands on its head and you confess the mistake you made. Then you slaughter the cow. It's butchered in front of you. The blood is poured on the altar. The fat is put on the altar to burn. How do you feel? (Don't say disgusted.) I'll tell you how you feel. You feel overwhelmed with emotion, jarred by the confrontation you've just had with death, and grateful to be alive. You've had a catharsis. The cow on the altar was a vicarious offering of yourself.

Sound barbaric?

No more so than the ways we customarily use animals already. We routinely eat animals, wear them, turn them into furniture, use them for medicinal research, and hunt them for sport. God created animals for our use (though not for wanton abuse). The need of someone who is oppressed by guilt to restore his relationship with God is just as legitimate as the desire for a dinner that's "finger lickin' good."

The Hebrew word for "sacrifice" is *korban*. The root *karev* means to "draw close." Sacrifices are to help us draw close to God.

I Did It My Way

When the Tabernacle is finished, there are seven days of celebration. On the eighth day the Children of Israel put a sacrifice on the altar.

*A great ball of fire descends from the heavens and consumes the
offering. The people are overwhelmed with excitement and emotion.
They know God is in their midst. Then two of Aaron's sons, Nadav and
Avihu, filled with ecstatic desire for even greater closeness to God, take
incense and rush into the Tabernacle—and God strikes them dead.
The Children of Israel are stunned.*

(Leviticus 9:1-10:2; pp. 589-593)

Why does God do this?

The Bible's only clue to Nadav and Avihu's crime is the Bible's
words that "they brought an offering God had not commanded."
But what's wrong with volunteerism?

Did you ever notice that kids are models of helpfulness at a
friend's house but won't pick up their socks at home? It's easy
to be good when you don't have to, because there's no obligation to make you feel trapped and resentful. But when
you're expected to clear the table, it gets your back up, and
then being good is an altogether different and greater challenge.
Goodness that comes and goes on a whim is neither meaningful
nor reliable. Real goodness is accepted as an obligation.

Autonomy from constraint is a core American value. Pilgrims
seeking religious freedom settled the thirteen original colonies, and
flight from political and religious coercion continues to fuel immi-
gration to the United States.

But exaggerated emphasis on autonomy has a dark side—the
breakdown of community and of moral obligation. A father needs
to come home and feed his kids every night, even though he
doesn't always feel personally rewarded. If each person's priority
is only his own fulfillment, you can't count on anyone.

Nadav and Avihu don't just value autonomy. They make individuality the guiding principle of their lives. (The word *nadav*
means "voluntary.") They feel like making an offering, and they
want to do it their way. But if you want to get close to God, you
have to do it *His* way.

God Stuff

In an alternate explanation of their crime, the Talmud suggests Nadav and Avihu's religious ecstasy actually came from being drunk—antithetical to the Bible's insistence that only clear-headed rationality can be the basis of true spirituality.

After Nadav and Avihu die, Moses says to Aaron, "This (their deaths) is what God alluded to when He said 'on the day the Tabernacle is set up, I will be sanctified through [the deaths of] those who are close to me.'"

(Leviticus 10:3; p. 593)

This AFFECTS YOU

Moses consoles Aaron by telling him the death of Nadav and Avihu will cause the Israelites to deepen their relationship with God. He tells him that this gives meaning to his children's deaths.

Our individual lives are part of the great tapestry of our nation's unfolding relationship with God. Just as a piece plucked randomly from a 1,000-piece puzzle is meaningless out of context, so the meaning of our own lives—and deaths—is expressed and understood only in relationship to the history of the Jewish People.

These events take place on the eighth day after the Tabernacle is finished. The number seven symbolizes the natural world. Eight symbolizes the transcendent. On the eighth day after birth, a baby is circumcised and brought into the covenant with God. On the fiftieth day after leaving Egypt, the Israelites received the Torah. (The fiftieth day is the beginning of the eighth week.) When the menorah burned for eight days at Hanukkah, the Jews knew they were witnessing a miracle.

Zebra Steaks Are Out

Some foods are permissible for the Israelites to eat, while others are prohibited. The permitted ones are called kosher.

✦ *All plants are kosher (which doesn't mean they're all healthy to eat, or taste good).*

✦ *Fish are kosher if they have fins and scales (Catfish and sharks, for example, are out.)*

✦ *Animals are kosher if they have split hooves and chew their cud (which means they regurgitate their lunch and eat it again. kosher doesn't always mean appetizing.)*

✦ *Carnivorous birds are not kosher.*

✦ *In general, reptiles and insects are out, but some species of grasshoppers are kosher. (Do I hear you salivating?)*

(Leviticus 11:1-31; pp. 597-603)

Though it is popularly believed that the rationale for the Biblical dietary laws is their health benefit, this is a misconception. Why then does it matter what we eat?

The logic of some commandments is obvious. Every society prohibits murder and theft. But the rationale for other commandments is not so obvious. The commandments whose reasons are obscure to us are called *hukim*. The word *hok* means "boundary." In the Psalms, for example, it says that God made a *hok*, a "boundary," for the sea. Because our desires for food, sex, money, power, and honor are unlimited, we need boundaries.

There is a short story by Tolstoy called "How Much Land Does a Man Need?" The story goes like this:

The devil decides he is going to destroy a particular peasant, using the peasant's lust for land. He draws him on and on, always with the promise of owning more and more land. Finally, the peasant hears of a place far out to the east, where the people are so simple-minded, they will give you all the land you want for nothing, so he goes there.

"Sure," they say. "You can have as much land as you can walk around in the course of a day."

The man gets up early and starts to walk. As he goes on, he sees more and more land he wants. As mid-day comes, he realizes he has gone too far to return by sunset, and he begins to run. He runs faster and faster, and finally, just as the sun sets, he throws himself across the finish line, and then he has a heart attack and dies.

They pick up a shovel and bury him. It was exactly six feet from his head to his feet. It was all the land he needed.

Raise 'em Right

Without boundaries we destroy ourselves.

One of parents' key roles is to set boundaries for their kids. But the location of the boundary is always arbitrary.

"8:30," I say to my kids, "it's bedtime."
"Why isn't bedtime 9:00?" they ask.
"Great question," I say. "Why isn't bedtime 8:00?"

The laws of *kosher* are God's way of setting boundaries for us and for our appetites.

The Bible identifies the pig as the only animal in the world with split hooves that doesn't chew its cud. Now remarkably enough, this is true. How could Moses know that? He was never on the Siberian Steppe or the South American pampas. He goes out on a limb to make a claim he can't possibly verify, and he's right! It's a piece of evidence that the Bible could only have been written by God.

Out, Out, Damn Spot

Certain experiences make us tumeh, or "unclean."
Contact with death is the paradigm of tumah, which is why we wash
our hands when we leave a cemetery.
A woman is tumeh, when she gives birth or has her period.
(Leviticus 12:1-15:33; pp. 609-635 and
Numbers 19:11-22; pp. 841-843)

umah has nothing to do with dirt.

When the soul lifts the body and connects it to a higher purpose, that's holiness. When the body overwhelms the soul and drags it down, that's *tumah*. The psychological experience of *tumah* is depression and hopelessness—the feeling that nothing we do matters or lasts.

Many years ago I went to the funeral of a great scholar. As his body was lowered into the grave, one of his arms slipped outside the shroud. I was seized with despair at the sight. What's the point of living, I felt, if in the end you're just a hunk of dead meat?

Similarly, during pregnancy, a woman may find that her body's needs assert themselves so loudly and aggressively that she loses all sense of her own identity.

We "cleanse" ourselves of *tumah* by going to a ritual bath or *mikvah*. The *mikvah* is an opportunity for spiritual rebirth and renewal. (It wasn't the spot on her clothes that bothered Lady Macbeth. It was the stain on her soul.)

This AFFECTS YOU

The laws of *tumah* have an important side benefit. They help keep sexual passion strong in married life.

Let's say your favorite dessert is ice cream. The first night you eat it, you're very happy. The next night, you're still pleased. The third night, you decide to pass on the dessert. By the end of the month, even rice pudding looks good.

Sexual boredom afflicts the best of marriages. But how can one partner suggest a moratorium without hurting the other's feelings?

When a woman menstruates, she and her husband refrain from sexual relations. Though the days of abstinence are sometimes difficult, each month a great river of passion is channeled back into the couple's sexual relationship.

The Heartbreak of Psoriasis?

The Bible speaks of a disease called tzaras.

(Leviticus 13:1-14:57; pp. 609-629)

*T*zaras is sometimes translated as "leprosy," but it was really an affliction signaling a spiritual illness. People got *tzaras* if they spoke slander. (We talked about slander, or *loshan hora*, in discussing the ninth of the Ten Commandments.)

Life isn't lived alone, it's lived with others. If through slander we destroy our community's atmosphere of trust, we destroy our own ability to live fully. If you got *tzaras*, you learned that when you speak slander, the life you destroy is your own.

After the death of Nadav and Avihu,
God tells Moses that Aaron should perform the Yom Kippur services.
It is his job to intercede for the Israelites with God,
bear their prayers aloft, and seek forgiveness
for their transgressions.
The central event of the service involves casting lots (like dice) on two
identical goats. One goat is then sacrificed and its blood sprinkled in the
Tabernacle's innermost sanctum, the Holy of Holies.
The other goat becomes the "scapegoat."
Aaron places his hands on it and confesses the Nation's mistakes.
The scapegoat is then thrown over a cliff,
symbolically bearing the guilt of the people on its head.

(Leviticus 16:1-28; pp. 637-645)

The Right Man For the Job

*T*wo men may be identical in genes, upbringing, and experience. One sanctifies his life, and uplifts the world around him. The other destroys himself, and drags the world down with him. This is the miracle of free will.

Psychologist Victor Frankl survived the Nazi death camps. He points out that in the camps some people became monsters and others became saints.

Pain embitters some people; their misery taints the lives of all around them. Pain deepens other people; they grow and enhance the lives of everyone they know. Whatever the circumstances of our lives, we still have choice. That is the meaning of "free will."

The two Yom Kippur goats begin identical. Then one ascends to the highest level of holiness, while the other is identified with the deepest shame.

Though Aaron's loss might have embittered him, instead it made him a greater, deeper, better person. Having demonstrated in his own life the power of free will, Aaron could now lead the Israelites toward a greater intimacy with God on Yom Kippur.

I n my experience the moment of tragedy is no time for philosophy. All our energy goes into coping, and getting though the day. Eventually the pain recedes, and then looking carefully, we may find that tragedy has left behind gifts of insight into the meaning of our lives.

Some years ago, my baby daughter was diagnosed with cancer. All my friendships were tested in the crucible of those terrible days when we first discovered and began to deal with her illness. I began to value simpler qualities in my friends than I did previously. Caring seemed more important to me than brilliance—and far more rare. At a time when I needed it badly, there were few people who took the time to involve themselves in my life and offer their support. I judged harshly those who didn't make the offer until I considered whether I would have behaved differently myself. When I realized that I would have acted the same way, what I valued about myself began to change.

Those qualities I had previously thought most precious and important—my intelligence, ambition, and creativity—were completely unimportant to me in my crisis, useless to help my baby or even to help myself. It was unimportant whether I was cultured or well read or whether my friends were interesting and important. It didn't matter whether I knew more or less than others or who was more successful. I realized how often I had failed others through preoccupation with my own talent, so much less important than my ability to care.

These simple lessons seem to me so important, so close to the heart of life, that I have come to embrace my own pain with a kind of tenderness. I think that through it, I may have gained what is best about myself.

Holiness Is How We Treat Others

✦ *Don't let your employee's wages remain with you overnight*

(Leviticus 19:13; p. 661)

If you tell the illegal alien you left to watch your kids that you'll pay her Friday, then you have to pay her Friday. "I'm running late. I'll pay you next week" is not an excuse the Bible countenances.

✦ *Don't place a stumbling block before the (morally) blind*

(Leviticus 19:14; p. 661)

"I was just following orders" is no excuse. Everyone is responsible for his own actions. But if you know that someone is naïve, and you encourage him to do something morally reprehensible, then you are also accountable.

✦ *Don't stand on your neighbor's blood*

(Leviticus 19:17; p. 661)

If people around you have bad manners, it's adequate to behave well yourself and to set a good example. But if what's going on is murder, and your response is limited to "not getting involved," then you are "standing on your neighbor's blood."

In a famous and horrible incident some years ago, a woman named Kitty Genovese was stabbed to death in the courtyard of a large apartment house. Hundreds of people watched, but no one called the police. They didn't want to get involved. Not doing evil is only part of virtue. You also have to prevent evil and do good.

✦ *Don't hate your neighbor in your heart—admonish him*

(Leviticus 19:18; p. 661)

If someone wrongs you, don't stew in your anger. Tell him you're mad and help him change. If you don't do this, you are culpable for your hatred. If you could have helped him to change but didn't, you also share responsibility for his behavior.

When the Romans were about to destroy Jerusalem, the Angel of Death asked God what to do with the good people of the city.

"Spare them," God said, "they didn't participate in the evil done there."

"It's true they didn't participate," the Angel retorted. "But they didn't do anything to prevent the evil from happening."

"I know that no one would have listened to them."

"*You* know that," the Angel agreed, "but *they* didn't know that."

"True," God said, "start with the good people."

✦ *Don't take revenge and don't bear a grudge*

(Leviticus 19:18; p. 661)

I ask to borrow your car and you say no. Then you ask to borrow my car and I say, "You must be kidding." That's revenge.

If I say, "You can borrow my car because I'm not a schnook like you," that's bearing a grudge.

✦ *Love Your Neighbor as Yourself*

(Leviticus 19:18; p. 661)

G rowing up in a Christian society, many people imagine "love your neighbor" comes from the New Testament. It's from Leviticus.

✦ Love means being truly attentive to someone else's needs, not just to your own pleasure.

One of my teachers, Rabbi Moshe Aaron Stern, told me that when he was a boy in yeshiva, his teacher found him at lunch one day, devouring a fish with great relish.

"Moshe Aaron," his teacher said, "you like the fish?"

"Oh yes! I love the fish!"

"Moshe Aaron," said the teacher, "if you loved the fish, you wouldn't eat it. You love yourself!"

✦ Love isn't just about emotion. It's about action.

"Emuna," I gushed to my wife one day, "I love you so much."

"Nachum," she told me, "less talk of love, more taking out of garbage."

✦ If you don't love yourself, you can't love anyone else either. (That's why the Bible says "love your neighbor *as yourself*.")

Real giving comes from a whole and healthy sense of self. The giving that is an attempt to buy other people's love isn't love at all. It's manipulation.

✦ *Don't crossbreed livestock*

(Leviticus 19:19; p. 663)

Huh? All these lofty ethical ideas and suddenly the Bible gets into animal husbandry?

Obviously you're more likely to love your neighbor if you don't crossbreed livestock than if you do. Why? It works like this:

I don't know why not to crossbreed livestock, but the Bible tells me not to, so I won't. I can't stand my neighbor, but the Bible tells me to love him. So I'll just have to go next door and see what he needs.

PART IV

Numbers
Journeying To The Promised Land

The fourth book of the Bible is called Numbers, because it starts with a census. This book resumes the story of the Israelites' journey through the desert. They run into many problems, but their biggest challenge is maintaining their own sense of hope and direction. Think of it as a metaphor for the journey of life.

If you ever found raising children challenging, pity Moses – he has a whole nation to shepherd through the desert. If you want a map of life's pitfalls, start here.

CHAPTER 11

A Funny Thing Happened On The Way To Canaan

Immediately after giving the Ten Commandments God tells the Israelites to organize themselves by tribe and take a census.

(Numbers 1:1-54; pp. 727-733)

Isn't living in tribes sort of—well—tribal?

It's politically correct to insist that everyone is the same—Jews, gentiles, men, women, blacks, whites, Irish, Chinese—a whole rainbow of colors swirled into one great gray stew of uniformity. But how drab! The Bible's position is vive la différence!

Every nation, every tribe, every person has something unique to offer. We contribute most when we maintain our individuality.

The last time my daughter had an earache, I took her to the doctor. Before examining her, the doctor (a Jew) said to me, "You know why I don't like religion?" (This is the pitfall of my job. My three-year old is screaming and suddenly I'm involved in a seminar on religion.)

"No, I don't know. Why don't you like religion?"

"Because it's parochial. When I go out with my friends, one's Chicano and one's Filipino, and I think that's the way it should be."

"The problem," I told him, "isn't that your friends are Chicano or Filipino. The problem is that since you don't know anything about your own religion, you're the only one at the table with nothing to offer. Now please check her ears."

If the differences between men and women were merely physical, marriage wouldn't be so rewarding. But marriage offers a special opportunity for emotional growth and discovery precisely *because* men and women are so different.

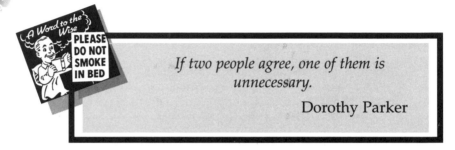

> *If two people agree, one of them is unnecessary.*
>
> Dorothy Parker

Each of the twelve tribes has a banner, and this is the origin of flags.

It All Starts With the Home

Families compose the tribes, and tribes compose the nation. The Book of Numbers began by discussing the tribes. It now switches to discuss the family and the basis of the family—marriage.

Marriage can't survive without trust. Even in the days of the Israelites, jealousy and suspicion sometimes poisoned marriages. The Bible's mechanism for restoring trust is called *mei sotah*, or "bitter waters."

A married woman goes alone to the home of a man she isn't married to. Her husband gets jealous and asks her not to do it again.
She does it again. The marriage is in jeopardy. They go together to the Tabernacle. The priest takes a parchment from the Bible and dissolves the ink into a cup of water, which the woman then drinks.
If she committed adultery, the woman and the man with whom she committed adultery both die. If she is innocent, she is unharmed, and

with this Divine testimony to her innocence, she and her husband
have a chance of living happily ever after.

(Numbers 5:11-31; pp. 753-759)

What if the woman suspects her husband of adultery?

Men aren't permitted to cheat on their wives either, but the commandment of *mei sotah* only applies to married women. Is that fair? I didn't write the Bible. I'm just telling you what it says. But experience demonstrates that while marriages sometimes survive a husband's unfaithfulness, they almost never survive unfaithfulness by the wife. Go figure it out.

Today, most marriage partners commit adultery at least once, and most marriages end in failure and divorce. Nobody believes he will be part of the statistics, but who wants to risk the odds? Here are some old-fashioned suggestions to improve your chances of staying married:

◆ Don't have sex until you're married.

I recently asked a group of young people whether they'd have sex with someone they weren't committed to.
"Sure," they said.
"Would you lend your car to a stranger?"
"Certainly not!" they said. (What a shocking suggestion!)
"Car—no. You—yes?"
"Sure," they said, "the car could get damaged."
The dings don't show, but if you have sex with people you're not committed to, you're going to get hurt. When you're hurt often enough, you become calloused and bitter, and then trust and intimacy become impossible.
Casual sex is a habit that's hard to break even once you get married. And even *before* you're married, sex often supplants attention to the issues of goals and character on which long-term happiness really rests. The cover of the book <u>Nice Guys Sleep Alone</u>

shows a couple passionately kissing. The balloon over the guy's head reveals what he is thinking: "This is wonderful. We should have lunch some time."

✦ When you *are* married, keep your sexual relationship private and exclusive.

In our sex-obsessed society, strangers hug and kiss like lovers, and every ad is adorned with pictures of semi-nude women. In such an environment, appetite—and jealousy—run wild.

If you don't want jealousy to taint your marriage, don't give it the opportunity. There's more to sexual intimacy than intercourse, and if you flirt with trouble, you'll probably find it.

✦ Remember that sex is about giving.

Here is a letter written in the twelfth century by a rabbi named Nachmanides, teaching his son how to make love to his wife:

"Begin with words that will draw her heart to you, and that will settle her mind, and make her happy—to unite her mind with your mind, and your intention with her intention. Tell her things that will produce desire, attachment, love, willingness, and passion, and that will draw her to fear of Heaven and a sense of piety and inwardness. Win her heart with words of charm and seduction and other proper things, so that both your intentions are united for the sake of Heaven. Don't have relations while [your] wife is sleepy, for then your minds will not be united. Do not hasten to arouse her desire, so that her mind may be serene. Begin in a pleasing manner of love, so that she will be sexually satisfied before you are."

Perhaps this all sounds quaint. But in the orthodox Jewish world, where these values are lived and taught, adultery is about as rare as murder. Maybe it's worth thinking about.

Bunch of Crazy Long-hairs

After the story of the sotah comes discussion of the nazir. This is a man who fears that his appetites dominate his judgment and vows not

to cut his hair and not to drink wine. Then at the end of thirty days,
he shaves his hair off and brings it to the Tabernacle.

(Numbers 6:1-21; pp. 759-763)

What's it all about?

Hair represents sensuality. (Ever see the movie in which the mousy girl lets her hair down and turns out to be Marilyn Monroe?) The *nazir* offers his hair to God as a symbol that he is sublimating and consecrating his sensuality and sexual energy. Alcohol also helps us "let our hair down," which is one reason we like to drink. But this guy is trying to get his libido under control, so he swears off wine for a month to help him recover his balance.

The Talmud says someone who saw a *sotah's* death should vow to become a *nazir*. But why is this necessary? Isn't her death adequate warning of the dangers of unfettered sensuality?

Even gruesome sights can become familiar. The first time a medical student sees a cadaver he vomits. The second time, he's less troubled. By semester's end, he eats lunch while he works and makes an ashtray of the skull.

Raise 'em Right

Divorce was once rare. Gradually we became accustomed to it, and now it's commonplace. Because we're no longer shocked, everybody's marriage is less secure. When you hear that someone you know is getting divorced, protect yourself by asking, "How will I make sure that never happens to me?"

Ditto—Not!

The head of each tribe makes a donation to the Tabernacle.
Each gives a silver bowl and a silver basin filled with oil and flour; a
golden ladle filled with incense; a young bull; six rams; six sheep;
six goats; and two cattle.

(Numbers 7:1-88; pp. 765-773)

The leader of each tribe makes exactly the same contribution, yet the Torah lists each separately. Couldn't it just say "ditto," and leave it at that?

Outwardly the donations were identical but because each donor's motivation and personality was unique, their gifts were distinct as well.

Individuality isn't about personalized license plates and exotic clothes. Individuality demands the far subtler and more difficult work of mining the resources of your own soul. If you do that, your individuality is vividly expressed in everything you do and say—even if you look the same as everyone else.

Spy Story (Sorry, No Stunts Or Nifty Cars)

The Israelites arrive at the border of the Land of Israel.
They send prominent men from each tribe as spies to explore how best to conquer the land. The spies spend forty days in Israel.
When they return, they bring back massive fruit as evidence of the Land's prodigal fertility. But they also warn that the land's inhabitants are fearsome and their cities heavily fortified.
The Israelites are disheartened. They cry and clamor to appoint a new leader to bring them back to Egypt.
God decrees that the Israelites spend forty years wandering in the desert (one year for every day the spies spent in the Land). Only when the generation that left Egypt dies will the next generation be permitted to enter the Promised Land.

(Numbers 13:1-44; pp. 799-811)

This is the tenth time the Israelites complain against God.

Why do they rebel against entering the Land?

A covenant with God is a great privilege. It's also a burdensome responsibility. After 210 years of slavery in Egypt and a trek through the desert, the Israelites are ready to kick off their shoes and have a beer. But when they hear the spies' report, they realize they will need God's ongoing help to conquer and settle the Land. At this point the burden becomes unbearable and even Egypt seems more attractive than living up to God's expectations.

The Jewish People traditionally viewed themselves as "a nation of priests" and "a light unto mankind." But the demands of this exalted aspiration are exhausting, and many Zionist pioneers hoped establishment of the State of Israel would permit Jews to live more normal lives.

> *"We must limit ourselves and forgo the rainbow of messianic*
> *dreams ... concede heavenly Jerusalem for the sake of the*
> *Jerusalem of the slums, waive messianic salvation for the sake of*
> *small, gradual reforms ... not 'the land of the heart' and not 'the*
> *divine city reunited,' ... but simply the State of Israel."*

(Amos Oz, In the Land of Israel)

But as the past fifty years seem to demonstrate, normal life is not available to the Jewish People.

The Israelites send spies to Israel, hoping to find a reason not to go into the Land.

Did someone ever try to convince you to do something you really don't want to do? You listen politely and ask sensible questions, but all the time your head is screaming, "No way! There is no way I'm going to do this!" That's the way the Israelites feel about going into the Land of Israel.

In 1938, Adolph Hitler threatened to go to war unless Germany received the Sudetenland, the industrialized strip of northern Czechoslovakia. England was treaty-bound to defend Czechoslovakia, but Britain's Prime Minister, Neville Chamberlain, went to Germany and acquiesced in this act of naked aggression. When Chamberlain returned to England, he was met at the airport by crowds delirious with joy. Chamberlain announced, "This means peace in our time."

One year later Germany invaded Poland, and the full futility and cowardice of Chamberlain's policy became apparent.

History has judged Chamberlain harshly, but it would have been impossible for anyone with the trust of the British people *not* to have made a deal with Hitler. The people didn't want to fight. That desire communicated itself to the country's leaders, and they found a way to give the people what they wanted.

The Children of Israel don't want to go into the Land. The spies are all great men, but social pressure sways the judgment of the best of us, and so the spies find reason to advise the people not to enter Israel.

Raise 'em Right

Until now, God endures the people's complaining pretty patiently. Why is His reaction suddenly so harsh and unforgiving?

God in His relationship with the Israelites is frequently mischaracterized as "the vengeful God of the Old Testament." But studies consistently indicate that children flourish best when raised in an environment that is neither permissive (all love) nor authoritarian (all discipline). Children need love and support. They also need clear boundaries and expectations, as well as predictable consequences for their actions.

If you use only love, you communicate "whatever you do is okay." You'll wind up with spoiled, selfish brats.

If you use only punishment you communicate "I hate you." You'll wind up with no relationship with your children.

God's patient nurture of the People through trials and difficulties clearly communicates His love. But the tenth time they rebel, God decides that without consequences, they will never learn.

Why did those who left Egypt have to die before the Israelites could enter Israel?

Military strategists are usually well-prepared to fight the last war. After 1918, the French built the Maginot Line, a series of fortified defenses well suited to the trench warfare of World War I. But these static defenses had no relevance to the blitzkrieg attacks of World War II. (When German tanks invaded Poland, the Polish cavalry rode out to confront them on horseback, with banners flying and trumpets playing. The results were predictably one-sided.)

The difficulty of adapting to changed circumstances isn't true in military affairs alone. The generation raised in Egyptian slavery couldn't adjust to the demands of freedom in the desert.

Forty years ago, American Jewry was menaced by Christian proselytizing and by "white-shoe" anti-semitism. Today, the threat to Jewish survival is apathy and assimilation, and the strategies of yesterday have little relevance to today's challenges.

Never Trust Religious People

Moses has a prominent cousin named Korach.
Korach begins to foment a rebellion. He circulates among the people,
accusing Moses of usurping power.
He asks the people, "Aren't we all holy? Didn't God speak to all of
us? Why have Moses and Aaron set themselves up
as intermediaries between the people and God?"

(Numbers 16:1-3; p. 821)

Korach's complaints appeared high-minded. His real grievance is that he covets Aaron's power.

From Korach to Khomeini, demagogues have the same selfish, greedy motives as the rest of us. But since their true motives are cloaked by lofty rhetoric, their potential for evil is far greater.

Nguyen Van Thieu, the dictator of South Vietnam, was a brutal, venal man, but normal life was possible in South Vietnam as long as you stayed out of politics. When the Communists took over, even wearing eyeglasses became a crime, and people fled in leaky rafts across shark and pirate-infested waters, just to get away.

When I was in yeshiva, one of the teachers fomented a rebellion against the administration. The head of the school remonstrated with him, "I don't understand how can you do this. You work for me!"

"I don't work for you," the teacher replied, "I work for God."

Beware of people who work for God.

> *I informed him [Lenin] that I could not cooperate with a regime that persecuted anarchists ... his reply was that my attitude was bourgeois sentimentality ... Russia was igniting the world revolution and here I was lamenting over a little blood-letting.*
>
> Emma Goldman

What happens to Korach? The ground opens up and swallows him alive. This effectively ends the argument.

(Numbers 16:31-35; p. 827)

What a Long Strange Trip It's Been

The deeper the Israelites go in the desert, the stranger things get.
Their next problem is a guy named Balak, the king of Moab.
Balak recognizes that with God on their side, the Israelites are too
tough to confront head on. He looks in the phone book under "Wizards"
and finds Bilaam. Bilaam's ad says: "Want someone cursed?
Call Bilaam! I know when God's mad."

(Numbers 22:2-6; p. 857)

What does this mean?

While the essence of God is constant and unchanging, God's personality is multifaceted. Consider an analogy:

We each have a core identity. Think of it as the "I" that has been constant throughout our lives. That core isn't usually evident to other people. (It isn't always evident to ourselves.)

Instead, people know us by our personality—the complex tapestry of qualities, strengths, and weaknesses expressed in our actions and choices in the world. (Watching me throw a ball, for example, you see whether I'm athletic. Watching me speak to my children you see whether I'm patient.) Neither athleticism nor patience define my essence. They are traits of my personality.

The world is literally created out of God's personality traits. We can describe water, for example as a combination of hydrogen and oxygen or, on a deeper level, we can describe it as a unique expression of God's kindness.

God's attributes aren't expressed uniformly in the world. That's why Jerusalem is "holy" and Las Vegas is "profane."

God's attributes are not expressed uniformly in time either. God's presence is expressed less at night. (That's why it's dark then.)

Bilaam knows the moment of the day when God is angry. He capitalizes on this knowledge to curse and destroy.

What is this? Voodoo?

We can identify people with their strengths and justify their faults. We can identify them with their faults and explain away their strengths. Bilaam hopes to capitalize on God's moment of anger to call attention to the Israelites' faults so God will destroy them.

But Bilaam doesn't realize that the Israelites are God's children. Even if you're angry with your children, you don't destroy them.

> *Rabbi Levi was the spiritual leader of a small town in Eastern Europe called Berditchev. Someone complained to Rabbi Levi that just outside the synagogue, still wrapped in his prayer shawl, a man was greasing his wagons' wheels.*
>
> *Rabbi Levi looked up to heaven. "Master of the Universe," he said, "do you see how wonderful your children are? Even when they grease their wagons, they wear their prayer shawls."*

Bilaam would pay for the opportunity to curse the Israelites. But when Balak's messenger arrives, Bilaam feigns humble piety. "Let me check whether God will let me curse the Israelites for you," he says. "Nope, sorry," he reports, "God doesn't want them cursed." This little game is repeated three times. Each time Bilaam humbly proclaims that he is bound by God's will. Each time Balak's messengers offer more money. Finally, God says to Bilaam, "If you want to do this, go ahead, but in the end you're going to say exactly what I want you to."

(Numbers 22:7-20; pp. 857-859)

IT's Simple

ike Laban and Ephron, who we met in the Book of Genesis, Bilaam seems righteous. He says the right words. But his true motives are cruel and mercenary.

In western movies, the villains are ugly and wear black hats. But in real life evil is not so obvious. It takes shrewd insight to distinguish between those who mouth pious slogans and those who really mean them.

Bilaam heads for Moab to meet Balak.
God sends an angel to warn Bilaam that God
isn't pleased with what he's doing. Bilaam's donkey sees the angel
standing in the road and turns aside. Bilaam hits the donkey and
forces it back on the path. Again the donkey turns aside,
and again Bilaam beats it. The donkey lies down in the road and
refuses to move. In a fury, Bilaam screams at the donkey and beats it.
The heretofore long-suffering donkey suddenly begins to speak:
"Hey! I don't normally do this. Why don't you open your eyes
and see what's going on."
Now Bilaam also sees the angel. The angel says to Bilaam, "Why
did you keep beating the donkey? If the donkey hadn't turned aside,
I would have killed you."
Bilaam says, "God told me it was okay to go to Moab,
but if you insist, I'll turn back."
God gives Bilaam up as a hopeless piece of work.
"Do whatever you want," He tells him,
and Bilaam continues toward Moab.

(Numbers 22:21-35; pp. 859-863)

Why doesn't God stop Bilaam?

When I was twenty years old and a junior at Yale University, I took a trip to Israel. I visited a school called Aish HaTorah, where for the first time I encountered traditional Jewish study of  God Stuff

the Bible. At Aish HaTorah, I thought I would learn more important lessons about living than I had at Yale, so I decided to drop out of college. I called my parents to tell them, though I didn't think they would like it. To my great surprise, my father didn't argue. Instead he told me, "You're an adult. You have to decide what you want to do with your life, and do it."

It was a terrifying moment. But it was also the greatest present my father ever gave me. His words told me, "I trust you. I believe you can make important decisions for yourself."

Animals do precisely what they're created to do. Only human beings have freedom. Freedom to define ourselves is the dignity and the greatness of being human. But freedom brings risk. We can uplift ourselves and uplift the world. We can also destroy.

God lets Bilaam choose his own course, and Bilaam's choices destroy him.

> *When Bilaam gets to Moab, Balak takes him to a hill from which he can see the Israelites' encampment. Bilaam tries to curse them, but a blessing comes out instead. Balak takes Bilaam to a different spot, with the same result. The third time Bilaam opens his mouth, he prophesies the coming of the Messiah and the ultimate downfall of the nation of Moab.*
>
> (Numbers 22:36-24:25; pp. 863-875)

Whoa! Did you say *"Messiah"*?

One of the Bible's basic tenets is that the world will change. The greed, violence and self-interest that dominate the Earth will be supplanted by love and by the pursuit of truth. The catalyst for this change will be the *Messiah*, which means "the anointed one." The *Messiah* isn't God or the "son of God." He will be a king from the tribe of Judah.

This concept exercises profound influence on our world.

At the United Nations, otherwise practical people spend their time working for universal peace and disarmament. Though this may seem "the impossible dream," they are inspired by a quote from the Book of Isaiah, written on the United Nations' wall:

"They shall beat their swords into plowshares, and their spears into pruning hooks: nation shall not lift up sword against nation, neither shall they learn war any more."

From popular to highbrow culture, the idea of redemption and rebirth shapes our world view:

✦ Popular movies (like E.T.) frequently evoke longing for a simpler, richer, and more rewarding life—a life we sense may not be permanently lost.

✦ Sigmund Freud saw Man in conflict with himself—torn between the libidinous passions of the id, and the "dos" and "don'ts" of the super ego—a picture of permanent conflict and misery, but don't despair! By learning to sublimate the id's power, Man will be transformed into a free being! The very nature of our life, in other words, will change.

✦ Karl Marx's economic treatise, <u>Das Capital</u>, goes through a long sober analysis of the relationship between capital and labor. But sober analysis takes a sudden impassioned turn as Marx prophesies a time when "workers will recognize their brotherhood," and work for the common good, not personal profit.

Though often disguised in secular clothes, longing for the advent of the Messiah permeates our culture.

Back in Moab, Balak is not pleased that he's paid Bilaam to bless his enemies so he sends him away. Before leaving, Bilaam gives Balak some parting advice on how to destroy the Israelites.
"This people's strength is their relationship with God, and that depends on the moral quality of their lives. If you corrupt them morally, your job is half-finished."

Balak thinks this is great advice. He convinces the Midianites to prostitute their daughters to seduce the Children of Israel. A plague begins among the Israelites. (It is God's way of saying "I'm really not pleased with you.")
An Israelite named Zimri waltzes his Midianite floozy (her name is Cozbi) right past Moses and into his tent. A man named Pinchas, from the tribe of Levi, follows Zimri and Cozbi into their tent, and stabs them both to death. The plague ends.

(Numbers 25:1-9; p. 875)

What kind of lesson for living is this?

We discussed *kina*—zealous anger, in the Genesis story of Shimon and Levi's destruction of the village of Shechem. Like any character trait, zeal can be used for good or evil. And as we noted earlier, it's easy to commit terrible crimes and mask your violence with pious rhetoric. But anger is part of the arsenal of our emotions, and there are times when it's the only tool that works. Pinchas' outrage jolts the Israelites back to their senses. Think of it as smashing a vase to startle drunken revelers into awareness of their actions.

The plague ends and God orders another census of the Nation. (This makes the third time. What can I say, He loves them.)

(Numbers 26:1-51; pp. 879-883)

Seasons of the Soul

The Bible lists the holidays that will become a permanent part of the Jewish calendar.

Holidays are opportunities for personal growth woven into time. Like a circular staircase, winding continually around and around in ever-higher planes, each year brings us the same opportunities in a spiral toward eternity.

✦ **Passover**—*Passover commemorates the exodus of the Children of Israel from Egypt in the year* 2448 (1313 B.C.E.)

Jews calculate dates from the time of Adam, the first human being with a soul. Instead of using "B.C." ("before Christ") or "A.D." *Anno Domini* ("year of our Lord"), Jews refer to dates on the non-Jewish calendar by the notations "B.C.E." ("before the common era") or "C.E." ("common era").

The opportunity of Passover is freedom.

Freedom is not acquired only once. It needs to be continually learned and reacquired. You can be free in a prison cell and a slave in a free country for true oppression comes from within oneself.

Self-concern is enslaving. Preoccupied with my own needs or with others' opinions, I am a slave to constant anxiety. A man who can't stop smoking isn't free, nor is one terrified of pain or rejection. (In Fear No Evil, Natan Sharansky tells of a Soviet prisoner the KGB manipulated through his caffeine addiction.)

For Passover we clean the leavened bread from our homes. Leaven symbolizes ego: Pompous (filled with hot air) but insubstantial, it's all show and no substance. (In The Informed Heart, Bruno Bettelheim reports that the rich collapsed most quickly in the concentration camps of World War II. Stripped of comfort and social position, they had little self to fall back upon.)

Matzo is "poor man's bread." It isn't fancy and makes no pretenses. Simple and nourishing, it represents freedom. *Matzo* is a way of being, and eating *matzo* is the way we internalize its lesson.

Passover falls in spring—the time when the first buds of the season's new growth appear. Spring's feeling of rebirth and joyous opportunity complements the holiday's invitation to seize anew the opportunity of our lives.

The events of Passover are covered in the first 15 chapters of the Book of Exodus. Observance of the holiday is mandated in Exodus 23:15 and 34:18 and in Deuteronomy 16:1.

✦ **Shavuot**—*Shavuot commemorates the Israelites' receipt of God's commandments at Mount Sinai, fifty days after the exodus from Egypt.*

At Passover we achieve the freedom and independence to create our lives. But freedom is mere absence of constraint. That's not enough to make life valuable. A full and passionate life demands meaning—a reason for living.

Fifty days after the exodus, the Children of Israel use their freedom to bind themselves to the joy, the passion, the demands, and discipline of a covenant with God. This is the holiday of Shavuot.

Shavuot falls in late Spring to early Summer—the time when the season's first fruits appear. After a cold and fallow winter, the first fruits are particularly precious. But after 230 years of slavery, the Israelites pledged the first fruits of their freedom to God. (Without, for example, first spending a long weekend relaxing on the beach in Miami.)

In extreme circumstances, it is impossible to survive without meaning.

Solzhenitsyn makes this point repeatedly in his account of the Soviet prison camps, <u>The Gulag Archipelago</u>. It is *the* point of Victor Frankl's story of survival in Auschwitz, <u>Man's Search for Meaning.</u>

The events of Shavuot are described in Exodus chapters 19-20 and reprised in Deuteronomy chapter 4. Observance of the holiday is commanded in Exodus 34:22 and Deuteronomy 16:19.

✦ **Succot**—*Hotels in the desert are few and far between. The Children of Israel live in fragile booths, called* succot, *which leave them vulnerable and intimately dependent on God. In commemoration we move out of our houses for a week to eat and sleep in backyard* succot.

Throw out the home entertainment center. The holiday of *Succot* affirms that the sweet intimacy of a relationship with God is all we need.

    Succot comes at harvest time. On Succot we harvest a year of spiritual insights. The sense of prosperous well-being that attends the gathering of the crop complements our delight and satisfaction in our intimacy with God.

Observance of Succot is commanded in Exodus 34:16 and Deuteronomy 16:13.

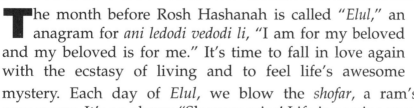

✦ **Rosh Hashanah**—*Rosh Hashanah is the beginning of the New Year, literally "the head of the year," the day we stand in judgment for the year just passed.*

The month before Rosh Hashanah is called *"Elul,"* an anagram for *ani ledodi vedodi li,* "I am for my beloved and my beloved is for me." It's time to fall in love again with the ecstasy of living and to feel life's awesome mystery. Each day of *Elul,* we blow the *shofar,* a ram's horn, in synagogue. It's an alarm: "Sleepers arise! Life is passing you by!"

    On Rosh Hashanah we pray repeatedly for life. But to justify a new year, we need to account for the year past. Did we actively live our time—filling it with growth, insight, and caring for others? Did we waste it?

    What *could* life be? Rosh Hashanah gives us the chance to renew our vision for the coming year.

Observance of Rosh Hashanah is commanded in Leviticus 23:23 and Numbers 29:1.

Rosh Hashanah comes in early fall.

✦ **Yom Kippur**—*The original Yom Kippur is the day God forgave the Israelites for worshipping the golden calf. On Yom Kippur we ask forgiveness for our mistakes.*

We all make lots of mistakes. We hurt people we love. We squander our time. We become alienated from God. The weight of accumulated failure is a depressing burden. It pushes us toward the worst mistake of all—despair.

But God doesn't expect perfection. He expects responsibility. If you broke something, fix it. If you hurt people, apologize. Don't waste time wallowing in pain and guilty self-abuse. Regret lost opportunities, take responsibility for your mistakes, and try again.

The freedom to re-create our lives is almost unlimited. This story appears in <u>Hasidic Tales of the Holocaust</u>:

With a promise of better treatment, Jews in the concentration camps sometimes served as *kapos,* "labor bosses." They were famous for their murderous brutality.

It was the day before Yom Kippur. A group of prisoners desperately wished to observe the holiday, perhaps for the last time. They asked Rabbi Israel Spira to intercede with Schneeweiss, a notoriously brutal *kapo.*

At the risk of his life, the rabbi went to Schneeweiss.

"You are a Jew like me," he said. "Tonight is the eve of Yom Kippur. There is a small group of young Jews who wish to observe the holiday. It means everything to us. It is the essence of our existence. Can you do something about it? Can you help?"

"Tonight I can't do a thing," Schneeweiss said. "But tomorrow, on Yom Kippur, I will do for you whatever I can."

The next morning he took the prisoners to the office of the SS.

"You will shine the floor without polish or wax," said Schneeweiss. "And you, Rabbi, will clean the window with dry rags, so you will not transgress any of the major categories of work [forbidden on the holiday]."

Then he left.

The rabbi stood on a ladder, with rags in his hand, cleaning the huge windows, chanting the prayers. His companions stood on the floor, polishing the wood and praying with him.

"All of them are beloved, pure and mighty. All of them in dread and awe do the will of their Master. All of them open their mouths in holiness and purity, with song and psalm, while they glorify and ascribe sovereignty to the name of the Divine King."

Around twelve o'clock the door opened, and like angels of death, two SS men came into the room. They brought a cart of food.

"Noontime," one announced. "Time to eat bread, soup, and meat. Eat immediately, or you will be shot!"

None of the Jews moved.

The soldiers called Schneeweiss.

"Schneeweiss, if these Jewish dogs refuse to eat, I will kill you with them."

"It is Yom Kippur, the Day of Atonement. They are not permitted to eat."

The German pointed his revolver at the kapo's head.

"I said eat."

The kapo stood erect.

"It is Yom Kippur. We won't eat."

And the German shot him dead.

If even Schneeweiss was capable of such greatness and courage, what could we make of *our* lives?

Yom Kippur comes nine days after Rosh Hashanah. It is mandated in Leviticus 16:29 and 23:26.

The following holidays became part of the Jewish calendar after Moses' death and the Bible's end.

✦ *Tisha B'Av—The day the spies dissuaded the Israelites from entering Israel was the ninth day of the month of Av. It has been a day of national calamity ever since. Despair, the Bible teaches, sows the seeds of disaster.*

On the ninth of *Av* in 3338 (423 B.C.E.), Nebuchadnezzer destroyed the Temple in Jerusalem and sent the Israelites into exile in Babylon. Seventy years later the Jews returned and rebuilt the Temple. It was destroyed by the Romans in 3830 (70 C.E.), on the ninth of *Av*.

On the ninth of *Av* 1492, the Jews were expelled from Spain. World War I began on the ninth of *Av*, setting in motion a chain of events leading to the Holocaust.

In observance of *Tisha B'Av*, we fast. In a sign of mourning we sit on the floor, and read the <u>Book of Lamentations</u>, the prophet Jeremiah's account of Nebuchadnezzer's destruction of Jerusalem.

One night the Jews were chased from their barracks and into a field. In the middle of the field was a pit. Beside it stood SS and Ukrainian soldiers with machine guns.

The guards laughed drunkenly.

"You must jump over this pit. If you fail, you will die!"

The Rabbi Israel Spira moved toward the pit together with an atheist, with whom he had developed a deep friendship in the camp.

"Spira, we won't be able to make it. Why entertain them? Let us sit down at the pit's edge and die with dignity."

"My friend," said the rabbi, as they walked, "man must obey the will of God. If it was decreed from heaven that pits be dug and that we must jump, then pits will be dug and jump we must. And if, God forbid, we fail and fall into the pits, we will reach the world of Truth a second later. So my friend, we must jump."

As they came to the edge, the rabbi closed his eyes and commanded in a powerful whisper, "We are jumping."

When they opened their eyes again, they found themselves on the other side.

The atheist grabbed the rabbi and burst into tears.

"Spira, we are here! We are here, and we are alive," he said. "Tell me, rabbi, how did you do it?"

"I was holding on to my ancestral merit. I was holding on to the coattails of my father, my grandfather, and my great-grandfather. I held onto Abraham and Isaac and Jacob," said the Rabbi. "And you my friend, how did you reach the other side of the pit?"

"I was holding on to you," the man replied.

The long night of our exile has been filled with suffering, loss, and blood curdling terror. An intimate relationship with our history has given us the ability to survive.

It is said Napoleon was once passing through the streets of Paris when he heard Jews crying inside a synagogue.

"Why are they crying?" he asked.

"They are crying for the Temple's destruction 1700 years ago."

"A people that remembers the Temple's destruction for 1700 years will ultimately rebuild the Temple," said Napoleon.

The events of the first Tisha B'Av are described in the Book of Numbers, chapters 13 and 14.

Tisha B'Av comes in late summer.

✦ **Hanukah**—One thousand years after the exodus from Egypt, Alexander the Great conquered the Middle East and imposed Greek culture and religion on all the conquered nations. The Jews rebelled for religious freedom and fought a guerrilla war that lasted twenty-five years. In 3622 (138 B.C.E.), the Jews drove the Greeks from Jerusalem and rededicated the Temple, which the Greeks had turned into an idolatrous shrine. They found just one small flask of oil to light the menorah. But the flame, which should have lasted one day burned for eight, as though testifying that some ineffable power, had enhanced their efforts, with transcendent glow and power. We light candles in testament that faith makes miracles possible.

Hanukah comes in late December.

✦ **Purim**—During the Babylonian exile, in 3405 (356 B.C.E.), the Jews were threatened with genocide, but in an unlikely turn of events, their persecutors were destroyed instead. In commemoration, we read the Book of Esther. Then we don masks, have a feast, and get drunk. This is Purim.

The world of the Bible sometimes seems fantastic. The sea splits, the evil die, the righteous are rewarded. God is so active, and life is so orderly. The world of our experience seems very different. It's disorderly, unfair, and cruel. God is concealed.

The salvation of Purim involved no overt miracles. God's hand was expressed through the mystery of chance, startling twists, and sudden opportunities.

Imagine the terror of being lost and vulnerable. Then imagine the relief, shock, and joy of discovering that you were never lost. God was caring for you even when you thought you were most alone. It's peek-a-boo on a grand scale. Purim gives us courage to have faith in a world where God is hidden.

Purim comes in early spring.

Back to our story. God tells Moses that after his death, Joshua will succeed him as leader. Then God describes to Moses the boundaries of the Land, and the narrative ends of the Israelite's journey.

(Numbers 27: 18-22; p.884; 34: 1-15; p. 923)

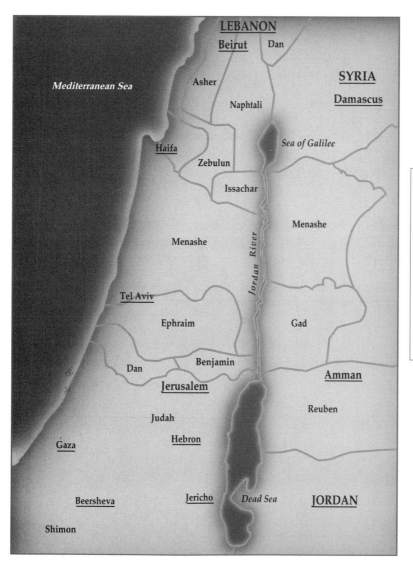

The division of the Land of Israel amongst the twelve tribes. <u>Underlined</u> names indicate present day countries and cities.

PART V

Deuteronomy
A Few Words Before We Part

The long journey is over. It is time for Moses to die and for the Children of Israel to enter the Land of Israel alone. Moses gathers the Nation and reviews their trek together through the desert. He underscores the lessons they have learned and highlights their mistakes. He exhorts them to seize the opportunities ahead and warns them of the challenges and dangers they will face.

Deuteronomy is Greek for "second law." Many commandments discussed earlier in the Bible are presented here for a second time. Deuteronomy is also the most abstract part of the Bible. If you want to understand the philosophy behind the Bible's commandments, start here.

CHAPTER 12

So Long, Farewell, Auf Weidersehn, Goodbye

We reprove people we love because we want them to be great. But since we're frustrated by their failings, we're prone to alienate them by continually harping on how they can improve. Moses didn't rebuke the people until the end of his life so he wouldn't drive them away with constant criticism.

IT'S Simple

Why isn't Moses going with the People into the Land of Israel?

Parents love their kids, so they tell them what to do: "Take your vitamins! Wear your boots! Don't touch the stove!"

But no one likes rules, and sometimes children are resentful of their parents' discipline.

The Children of Israel were resentful of God's demands. The umpteenth time the Israelites whined for water, God told Moses, "Take your stick. Speak to the rock, and it will give water."

HELP! I Need More Info

Moses went as he was told, but when the People screamed at him in rage and frustration, he lost his temper. He yelled at them and then he bashed the rock, which gushed forth water.

Only Man has the choice whether to listen to God. The mineral, vegetable, and animal worlds do exactly what they're created to do. God hoped that when the rock responded to Moses' gentle command, the people would introspect and become more responsive to God's will themselves. But inadvertently, Moses taught that even a rock resists listening to God, and gives water only when it's beaten.

The generation that left Egypt never truly appreciated that God loves them. Moses' mistake only reinforced their sense of grievance.

Because they never fully trusted God, they weren't allowed to enter the Land of Israel. Moses was their leader. He was responsible for them. And if they couldn't go in, he couldn't go in either.

Every time that Moses loses his temper, he makes a serious mistake.

What's the deal with the Land of Israel? Why not Uganda, for example, or maybe Brooklyn?

If there's one thing God hates, it's religion.

"Religion" usually means one day of worship sandwiched into a week's brutal exploitation of our neighbor. But God wants His commandments to shape every nuance of our lives—the way we do business, administer justice, fight war, make love, raise children, and respond to the poor. Only a community can live the Bible.

A community needs a place where it can live its ideals—it needs a land. And Israel is not just any land. It is a *holy* land, which means a place where God is uniquely present and available.

After the Six-Day War, Yitzhak Rabin, then chief of staff of the Israeli Defense Forces, is reputed to have said, "God had nothing to do with this victory."

Patton probably didn't comment on God's role in the Battle of the Bulge, but in Israel even atheists find God's presence too tangible to ignore.

An old joke tells of the Israeli prime minister's visit to the White House.

On the president's desk there are three phones. The president explains that the white phone is a direct line to the U.S. ambassador in Moscow. The red phone is a direct line to the commanding general of NATO. The blue phone is a direct line to God.

"But," says the president, "we never use that phone because it's too expensive."

Then the president goes to visit the Israeli prime minister. On his desk there are three phones. The prime minister explains that the white phone is a direct line to the Israeli ambassador in Washington. The red phone is a direct line to the head of the Army. The blue phone is a direct line to God.

"But how can a small country like Israel afford such a phone?" the president asks. "Even the U.S. can't afford to use it."

"Mr. President," says the prime minister, "here in Israel, it's a local call."

Shortly after the exodus, Moses set up a system of superior and district courts to help dispense justice. (This was actually Jethro's idea. We discussed it in Exodus.) Now Moses rebukes the people for their readiness to accept this plan.

(Deuteronomy 19:9-18; pp. 941-943)

Sounds strange. Moses set up the courts. Why is he upset that the people accepted them?

Moses reproves the people for their motive.

In medicine and science each generation knows more than the last. But God's commandments were communicated orally to Moses, from Moses to Joshua, from Joshua to the elders, from the elders to the prophets, and so on, to the rabbis of today. Each generation is further from the original source and struggles to recover what the last one knew. Had the people been truly eager to understand God's will, they wouldn't have agreed so readily to hear it second hand.

Don't Be a Wise Guy

Continuing his farewell, Moses explains concepts that are central to the proper observance of God's commandments.

✦ *Don't add to the Bible's commandments or subtract from them.*

(Deuteronomy 4:2; p. 959)

We sometimes imagine it's possible to fulfill God's intent while ignoring the letter of His commandments. The outcome is never good. God, it seems, knows best.

1. The Bible obligates a king to set boundaries for his own power and wealth. He isn't permitted too many wives, too many horses, or too much gold, "lest it turn his heart away from God."

King Solomon was "the wisest man who ever lived." He believed his wisdom would protect him from transgression, and he acquired wealth and wives without limit. But he was too wise for his own good, and in the end his wives led him into idolatry.

2. The Book of Kings records another striking example. (The Book of Kings is one of the latter books written by the prophets. It records events that took place several hundred years after the death of Moses.)

The prophet Isaiah comes to King Hezakiah and tells him, "You're going to die and then you're going to hell."

"What did I do wrong?" asks Hezekiah.

"You refused to fulfill the commandment to have children," says the prophet.

"But I saw prophetically my children would be evil!" says Hezekiah. "It's not your place to mix in God's realm," the prophet tells him. "You worry about your obligations, and God will worry about his."

3. The Reform movement originated with the belief that altered circumstances rendered the Bible's commandments obsolete. Beginning by discarding the dietary laws (clearly irrelevant, they argued, to a world with modern refrigeration) they waged a century-long campaign to replace the Bible's authority with human reason. The impact of that campaign appears in the following chart.

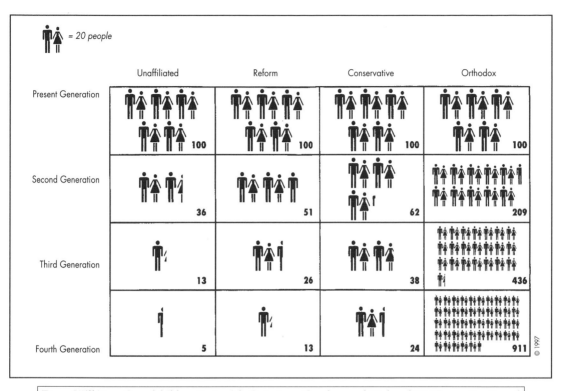

From *Will Your Grandchildren Be Jewish*, © Antony Gordon and Richard M. Horowitz. Based on the 1990 National Jewish Population Survey, the 1991 NY Jewish Population Study and quoted in <u>The Vanishing American Jew</u> by Alan M. Dershowitz and in *The New York Times*.

✦ *Never forget that you were present at Sinai. You saw the miracles in Egypt and at the sea. You heard God speak. Never stop communicating the experience of Sinai to your children.*

(Deuteronomy 4:9-13; p. 961)

Through the miracles of the exodus, the Israelites experienced God's care and intimate involvement in their lives. We remind ourselves of the exodus to establish the basis for faith and trust in God in our own lives.

God Stuff

A prominent rabbi, Rabbi Yaacov Kamenetzky was seated on a plane beside a secular biologist. Every few minutes, the rabbi's grandchildren appeared at his seat to ask if he needed anything.

"Your grandchildren are so solicitous," commented the biologist. "My own are far more aloof."

"My grandchildren think I'm two generations closer to Sinai," the rabbi answered. "Yours think you're two generations closer to the apes."

The Bible is a living tradition. Each Jewish parent and teacher links his children and students to the chain of tradition leading back to Mount Sinai.

✦ *Remember, you didn't see God at Sinai.*

(Deuteronomy 4:15-19; p. 963)

T he entire nation received prophecy at Sinai. Prophecy communicates God's expression in the world through visual metaphor. (A vision of a lion, for example, teaches that God's kindness is powerful and triumphant.) Moses wanted the Israelites to be clear that their visions at Sinai were expressions of God and insights into His will, but they were not visions of God. This may seem a distinction without a difference, but confusion about it leads to pantheism, or the worship of nature. Think of it as confusing a man with his hat.

✦ *The battle against assimilation is a constant struggle.*

(Deuteronomy 4:25; p. 963)

A relationship with God demands a constant pitch of intensity, but we'd rather fall asleep on the beach. Desire for freedom from the obligations and responsibilities of God's commandments leads to assimilation. The secular world celebrates retirement—release from obligation. Jewish life celebrates bar mitzvah—entry into the rigors and demands of the covenant.

There is a story of a king who becomes angry with his son and sends him far from the palace. The prince sets off again for home, but night falls and he is forced to stop. He awakens in the morning and becomes captivated by the beauty of the countryside. He decides to spend the day—and then another and another. He meets a young woman, falls in love, and marries. He gets a job and builds a house. He forgets about the palace.

The prince is the soul. The palace we are exiled from is our intimacy with God. The pleasures of the world call out to us "relax and enjoy yourself." We forget who we are and where we are going with our lives.

This is also the message of the world's most famous fish story —Jonah and the whale:

God tells Jonah to go to Nineveh and tell them that in forty days God will destroy the city. Instead Jonah goes to Jaffa, boards a ship, and sails for Tarshish. A great storm arises. Frightened, Jonah goes to sleep in the ship's hold. The sailors somehow recognize that Jonah is responsible for the storm. They throw him overboard and the sea becomes calm.

A great fish swallows Jonah. Then three days later God commands the fish to spit Jonah back out on dry land.

God tells Jonah, "Let's try it again. Go to Nineveh and tell them in forty days I will destroy the city."

The story is a metaphor for our struggle for clarity. Jonah is the soul. The soul is assigned to sanctify the world and draw it close to God. But we are seduced by the world's beauty. (Jaffa in Hebrew means "beauty.") The ship is the body, the sea is the world, and the storm is life's pains and troubles. God hopes confrontation with mortality will inspire us to examine our lives. But Jonah's response is the more common—we go to sleep (have a beer, turn on the television). The sailors throw Jonah overboard—this is death. The fish that swallows Jonah is the grave. Jonah is spat back upon the land—this is reincarnation. And the Almighty tells us to try again. "Go sanctify the world and bring it close to God."

Reincarnation?

Each of us is born with an opportunity and a challenge. We all have unique gifts to offer the world and unique challenges to perfect ourselves. If we leave the task unfinished the first time, we get a second chance, and then a third. But don't waste this one—it could be strike three.

> *Moses tells the people God won't permit them to abandon the covenant. He warns that if they violate the covenant they will be expelled from the Land of Israel. (A prophecy fulfilled not just once, but twice.)*

(Deuteronomy 4:26-27; pp. 963-965)

The title of a popular book may say I'm OK, You're OK, but if you really love someone, you don't permit him to sleep his life away. God loves the Israelites and He insists they rise to the potential of a holy and Godly life. When they opt for comfort, treat each other badly, or try to assimilate, God wakes them up again to the demands and opportunities of the covenant.

When Jews forget the covenant, non-Jewish nations remind them of it. Assimilation in Egypt brought anti-Semitism in its wake, a pattern repeated in Babylon, Greece, Rome, Spain, Germany, and the Soviet Union.

Anti-Semitism is no reason to walk with God. But it does invite us to examine the meaning of our identity. When you find that you inspire the world's most enduring hatred, you should probably wonder why. Here's Hitler's explanation:

The struggle for world domination is between me and the Jews. Everything else is meaningless. Jews have inflicted two wounds on this world: Circumcision for the body, and conscience for the soul. I come to free mankind from their shackles. (Rausching, The Voice of Destruction)

Can it be that our enemies know us better than we know ourselves?

A key element of living the covenant is how we treat each other. The following story appears in the Talmud:

There were once two brothers. One had a large family, and was very poor. The other was childless and very rich.

One day the rich brother thought to himself, "I have much more than I need, and my brother has many mouths to feed. I'll give him some of what I have."

In the middle of the night he took wheat from his field, carried it to his brother's field, and left it there.

The poor brother, meanwhile, thought to himself, "I have a large family, while my brother is all alone. He takes great pleasure in his wealth. I will give him some of what I have."

In the middle of the night he took wheat from his field, carried it into his brother's field, and left it there.

This went on for months until one night the two brothers ran into each other. Each was carrying wheat to the other's field. Instantly, they realized what had been happening. They fell upon each other and embraced.

On that spot, God decreed to build the Temple.

A Word to the Wise

PLEASE DO NOT SMOKE IN BED

The threat of internal disunity troubles me more than all the Syrian missiles.

Israeli Army Chief of Staff Amnon Lipkin-Shahak, quoted in the Israeli newspaper, Yediot Achronot, March 11, 1998

Moses particularly cautions the People not to relax their spiritual vigilance in times of prosperity.

(Deuteronomy 6:10-15; p. 975 and Deuteronomy 8:11-20; p. 985)

Troubles invite introspection, but when life is going well people devote little attention to self-improvement.

The United States has been an extraordinary haven for the Jewish People, providing unparalleled opportunity and security. But this very tolerance has also led to unparalleled assimilation.

A Word to the Wise

PLEASE DO NOT SMOKE IN BED

The Jews survived 2000 years of persecution in Europe. It's unclear whether they'll survive 100 years of tolerance in America.

◆ *Establish cities of refuge.*

(Deuteronomy 4:41-43; p. 967)

The Bible prescribes death as the penalty for premeditated murder (though, as indicated earlier, it was rarely applied). The penalty for manslaughter is exile to a city of refuge.

How is exile an equitable punishment for manslaughter?

The physicist Andrei Sakharov speculated that the secretiveness of Soviet society dramatically retarded the progress of science in that country.

Personal growth, creativity or scientific inquiry require meaningful interaction with other people. Isolation brings sterility. Exile is a taste of death.

IT'S Simple

God's justice aims at education, not angry vengeance. If you want to discipline your children effectively, never do it in anger. (Disciplining children in anger is called child abuse.) If your child runs into traffic, wait until you're calm. Say,

"I want to be very clear that you must *never* run into the street." Then hit him.

What is the commandment to establish cities of refuge doing in the context of all these lofty philosophical exhortations?

God warns the Children of Israel that assimilation will lead to persecution and exile. Perhaps He wants to reassure them that even in exile they will find refuge and ultimately they will return home.

> *Love God your Lord with all your heart, with all your soul, and with all your might. These words which I am commanding you today must remain on your heart. Teach them to your children and speak of them when you are at home, when you travel on the road, when you lie down and when you get up. Bind them as a sign on your hand, and let them be a reminder between your eyes. Write them on the doorposts of your houses and upon your gates.*
>
> (Deuteronomy 6:5-9; pp. 973-975)

This is the Shema. Jews say it every morning and evening. It is supposed to be the last thing we say before we die.

What does it mean to love God with *all your heart*? Not just the valves?

In Los Angeles there is a radio talk show called Religion on the Line. On the show, a Catholic priest, a rabbi, and a Protestant minister discuss religious issues. (This sounds like the opening of a joke, but it isn't.)

Once when I was the guest rabbi, the panel was asked, "If you'd had the chance, would you have killed Hitler in 1933?"

"No," the priest answered, "I would have loved him."

But I said, "I would cheerfully have shot him in the head."

Love and kindness are not always good, and righteousness isn't all saccharin sweetness. "Love God with all your heart" means be kind when it's appropriate, but don't forget the rest of the heart's emotions. Sometimes the right emotion is hate.

A Word to the Wise

PLEASE DO NOT SMOKE IN BED

There is a time for everything under the heaven:

A time to be born, and a time to die;

A time to plant, and a time to uproot plants.

A time to kill, and a time to heal;

A time to wreck, and a time to build.

A time to weep, and a time to laugh;

A time to wail, and a time to dance.

A time to scatter stones, and a time
to gather stones;

A time to embrace, and a time
to shun embraces.

A time to seek, and a time to lose;

A time to keep, and a time to discard.

A time to rend, and a time to mend;

A time to be silent, and a time to speak.

A time to love, and a time to hate;

A time for war, and a time for peace.

Ecclesiastes

What does it mean to love God with *all your soul*?

"Love God with all your soul" means be willing to die for God. This troubling idea needs explanation:

1. You don't know how precious something is until you know what price you'll pay for it.

Many years ago, a friend and I drove to the mountains in the middle of a Vermont winter. We stopped to change drivers and my dog hopped out of the car. A passing car brushed the dog which ran off terrified into the woods. It was midnight, and the temperature hovered near 0 degrees. We looked for the dog for hours in the freezing cold. All the time, I wondered to myself, How much does this dog mean to me? How long am I willing to do this for? (P.S. We found the dog.)

The Bible invites us to understand that our relationship with God is so precious, we would willingly to pay the ultimate price.

In the year 135 the Jews rebelled against Roman domination. The Romans crushed the rebellion with terrible savagery and then tried their best to stamp out Jewish life completely. They murdered every rabbi they could find and prohibited teaching Torah on penalty of death.

The next day Rabbi Akiba went to the marketplace and publicly taught Torah. He was arrested, sentenced, and tortured to death. As the executioner flayed Rabbi Akiba alive, he smiled and said, "All my life, I hoped for the opportunity to love God with all my soul."

The recognition that some things are worth dying for leads to the next point.

2. Being alive is not the greatest good.

Life is precious and it's wise to cling to it tenaciously. But life gains meaning from commitment to something *more* than life, and there is a time when *not* dying robs life of its meaning.

Rabbi Akiba's sacrifice was not in vain. His death, like the death of the Jews throughout history who died rather than convert, taught us the extraordinary importance of our relationship with God.

3. When you pay the ultimate price for something, it becomes more precious to you. It becomes *yours*.

Who has greater pride and pleasure in the State of Israel? Someone who risked his life to fight against impossible odds in 1948, or someone who wrote checks from the comfort and security of America?

Even kids understand this. In Dr. Seuss's *Horton Hatches the Egg*, an elephant named Horton is left to mind the egg of a frivolous bird named Mayzie. Through terrible troubles and at risk of his life, Horton protects the egg. When it finally hatches—it's an elephant with wings!

Invest yourself in something and it becomes yours. If you put yourself on the line for God and the Jewish People they become infinitely valuable to you. And *that* enriches your life beyond description. The opposite is also true: if there's nothing you're willing to risk your life for, there isn't anything you care about very much and *that's* a tragedy.

All the Torah's commandments yield to the preservation of life with the exception of three. If you're starving you can eat non-kosher food. If someone's life is at risk on Shabbat you immediately drive him to the hospital. But even to save your life, you can't worship idols, you can't commit incest or adultery, and you can't commit murder. (Self-defense isn't murder. It *would* be murder, however, if you saved yourself by killing an innocent bystander.)

What does it mean to love God with *all your might?*

Love God with "all your might" means treat your money and possessions as assets to make a difference and to bring the world closer to God.

A bumper sticker I've seen in Los Angeles reads "He who dies with the most toys wins."

But after we're warm, fed, and clothed, what *is* the point of all our toys? Possessions should be means not ends. What's the end? If having money doesn't serve some larger goal, having it is meaningless, and chasing it is destructive.

Separate tithes from your produce. ("Tithes" means "tenths.")
We spoke earlier about the commandment of tzedaka. In addition,
Moses tells the Israelites to tithe their crops to support the priests.
Another tithe is taken for eating in Jerusalem on the holidays.

(Leviticus 27:30; p. 723, Numbers 18:24; p. 837 and
Deuteronomy 14:22-28; pp. 1013-1015)

By tithing our income we sanctify our material life.

The priests teach the nation and bring it close to God. Supporting their work is no more than enlightened self-interest. (Education is the most important provision we make for our children's lives. But the miserly salaries paid teachers indicates clearly how little we actually value their work.)

Setting money aside to spend in Jerusalem guarantees we'll go there and uplift our lives.

A guy says to me, "I don't give charity. I'm selfish."

"You're not selfish," I tell him. "You're stupid. You think the greatest pleasure you can get from money is to eat it, drive it, or wear it. But you can also use it to create, to uplift yourself and the world, and to bring your life meaning."

If there should arise a prophet … and he does a miracle … and he says to you 'let us follow other gods,' do not listen to him. God is testing you to know whether you love Him with all your heart and with all your soul.

(Deuteronomy 13:2-6; p. 1007)

I met a Jewish girl who had converted to Christianity. She told me the following story in explanation:

I was critically ill in the hospital. The doctors gave up all hope for my recovery. A priest came. He told me to pray to Jesus. I prayed to Jesus and I recovered!
I told her, "Let me tell you a story."

Delegates of all the world's nations are gathered in the United Nations General Assembly. A man walks up to the podium.
'"Watch this," he says.
The United Nations building lifts off its foundation and hurtles into the sky. It lands on the moon. Delegates file out of the building and fill their pockets with moon rocks. The building flies back to Earth.
The man at the podium says, "Now I will reveal myself to you! I'm a frog!"
A frog? How can a man be a frog? That guy is powerful and dangerous, but he isn't a frog. He's crazy.
A man can't be god. Even if he has great power and does inexplicable wonders, he still can't be god, any more than a man can be a frog.
We're credulous creatures and easily impressed by things we don't understand. As Sky Masterson says in the movie <u>Guys and Dolls</u>:

"One day a guy's going to walk in and offer you a bet he can make the ace of spades jump out of a deck of cards in his pocket and squirt seltzer in your ear. But don't take that bet! Because if you do, you'll wind up with seltzer in your ear!"

Here Comes the Judge(s)

Appoint judges in all your cities … if a matter of judgment [or]
dispute arises in your cities—you shall rise up and ascend
to the place that God shall choose. You shall come to the judge who will
be in those days. You shall inquire and they will tell you
the word of judgment. You shall do according to the word that they will
tell you … and you shall be careful to do according to everything that
they will teach you … do not deviate from the word they tell you
to the right or to the left.

(Deuteronomy 16:18; p.1025; 17:8-11; pp. 1027-1029)

Since no written legal code could possibly cover all conceivable situations, judges must apply the Bible's laws to resolve specific cases. (We also discussed this in the context of explaining the oral law. See the sixth of the Ten Commandments.)

This raises a basic and important question. I'll listen to God. But why should I listen to the judges? They're only human, and they can make mistakes.

The short answer is that the Bible tells us to listen to the judges. The long answer ends the same way, but the middle is more interesting.

The Talmud tells of a disagreement in the Sanhedrin (the Jewish Supreme Court) over a point of law.

Of the 71 rabbis on the court, 70 say the law is one way. One holds the opposite view.

"If I'm right," the dissenter says, "let the walls of the study hall buckle inward."

The walls buckle.

"If I'm right," he says, "let the stream outside flow uphill."

The stream flows uphill.

"If I'm right, let a voice from heaven proclaim it!"

A voice booms out of heaven, "He's right!"

A rabbi from the opposing side gets to his feet.

"The Bible is no longer in heaven," he says. "The Bible tells us to follow the majority view. Miracles and voices from heaven are not admissible as evidence. You're outvoted and that's the end of it!"

When God gave the Bible and its explanation to Moses, it became our job to understand and apply it, and informed reason becomes the arbiter of the law's meaning.

This doesn't mean everyone's opinion of the law is equal, and it also doesn't make the final decision subjective or illegitimate. (People interpret and explain the laws of physics, but this doesn't make science subjective or illegitimate. And though scientists are people, not all people's opinions are equal. If I say, "Einstein was wrong. Really, $e=mc^4$," no one's going to listen. If Stephen Hawking says it, it means more.)

Why does the Bible say "come to the judge who will be *in those days*?" In the absence of time travel, what's the alternative?

This phrase means don't say, "I would have listened to Moses. But the rabbis of my time don't have that stature, so I won't listen to them."

I am a small guy, but through me, gentle reader, you are connected to my teacher and his teacher and his teacher—an

IT'S
Simple

> unbroken chain of tradition all the way to Mount Sinai. The teacher or judge in your day is the living link connecting you to God's revelation.

I played the game "telephone" when I was a kid. How do I know that over time the law hasn't changed from God's original intention?

In "telephone," the message is quickly corrupted because it's just a party game and the stakes are low. But imagine that the message we want to transmit is the cure for cancer. The reward for accurate transmission is enormous, and the price of failure is great. We'd be much more careful, and the message would come out the other end far more accurate. Cognizant of transmitting God's words, the sages of Jewish tradition transmit the oral law with exquisite care.

Why should I accept the authority of a 3300 year-old legal tradition?

A popular bumper sticker reads "Question Authority."

Mistrust of authority isn't new. Vietnam and Watergate may have heightened mistrust of government, but Enlightenment philosophers struggled against the authority of the church and state 200 years ago.

Blind allegiance to the past is stupefying. But tradition also gives us roots and it gives context to our lives. In denying tradition's claims we may just discover we have become orphans in history.

If I Were King of the Forest

When you come to the Land that the Lord your God gives you,
and you possess and settle it, you will say 'I want a king,
like all the nations of the world.

(Deuteronomy 17:14; p. 1029)

In democracies, government's legitimacy comes from the consent of the governed. That makes democracy the best government for a pluralistic society like our own. But in the homogeneous religious community of the Bible, legitimacy derives from the will of God. In that society, the ideal government is constitutional monarchy.

Princess Diana was the greatest celebrity of our generation. Her celebrity was partly a result of the (false) belief that wealthy, beautiful people lead more interesting and rewarding lives than the rest of us. It was also because she was a princess. Through their monarchs people participate in something larger than themselves—the nation.

The Hebrew word for "king" is *melech*. *Melech* also means "consult" or "unite." The king unites the disparate threads of individuals and knits them into a tapestry called "the People."

Colonel Mustard In the Library With a Candlestick

If a man is found murdered and there is no clue who committed the
crime, the elders from the nearest village bring a calf to a nearby
stream. They behead the calf. They wash their hands in the stream
and declare they are innocent of shedding the murdered man's blood.

(Deuteronomy 21:1-9; pp. 1043-1045)

There is no suspicion the village elders themselves committed murder. But they declare themselves innocent of guilt *by omission.* The responsibility of a community is to create an environment where our care for one another makes murder impossible.

All major cities have homeless populations. (Because many homeless people are schizophrenic, improvement of their lot is particularly difficult.) But a Jewish community embraces the homeless as its own. People speak to them by name on the street. They invite them in to their homes and give them food and clothing. By treating the homeless with dignity and not as trash, the community gives them back their humanity.

In the Great Depression, the scale of dislocation overwhelmed any individual community's capacity to respond. Only the Federal government could react on the necessary scale. But displacement of responsibility onto impersonal and distant government agencies is ultimately ineffective. More importantly, it deflects us from the opportunity to enrich our lives by caring for other people.

Acts of War

> When you go out to war against your enemies, and God delivers
> them into your hand ... and you see a beautiful woman
> and you desire her ... bring her to your house.
> She shall shave her head and let her nails grow.
> She shall remove the garment of her captivity from upon herself
> and sit in your house,
> and she shall weep for her father and her mother for a full month.
> Then you may come to her and live with her.
>
> (Deuteronomy 21:10-14; p. 1047)

In wartime otherwise decent people behave with extraordinary savagery. When society's thin moral veneer is punctured, a raging torrent of passion and terror sends life spinning over the edge. How do you save your own humanity in that environment of moral meltdown?

You don't dam a flood. You divert it.

You see a woman you want to rape? You can rape her. But first bring her to your home—in the familiarity of home, normal moral boundaries are reasserted. Let her shave her head and sit in mourning for a month—by month's end, the moment's passion has faded. And the intimate spectacle of the woman's grief has humanized her—she is no longer merely an object of sexual desire.

The next time you're enraged, tell yourself "I'm going to destroy this person. But first I'll give myself twenty-four hours to think it over."

The journalist Peter Maas offers the following terrifying paradigm for the war in Bosnia: Two people live peacefully as neighbors for forty years. Then one day one of them goes next door, shoots his neighbor in the head, and rapes his wife.

We're capable of all kinds of higher reason. We can split the atom and land a rocket on Mars, but sanity and civilization are a delicate edifice of reason over a maelstrom of envy, insecurity, and terror.

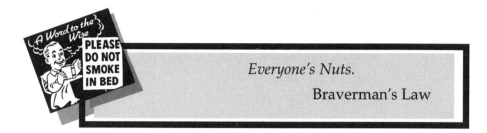

Everyone's Nuts.

Braverman's Law

One night, a guy is driving alone far out in the country. The bolts holding the wheels become loose, and eventually one wheel comes off. The car careens into a ditch.

With no phone or dwelling in sight, the driver is at a loss. Then looking up, he sees a fence with the sign "State Mental Institution." Behind the fence, a man with wild eyes stands frothing at the mouth.

"Take one bolt off each wheel," says the madman. Use them to fasten the fourth wheel, and you'll have three bolts on each wheel."

"That's brilliant," says the driver. "But tell me, if you're so smart, what are you doing in an insane asylum?"

"I may be crazy," says the madman. "But I'm not stupid."

That's all of us. We're not stupid. Just crazy.

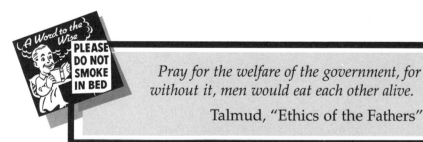

Pray for the welfare of the government, for without it, men would eat each other alive.

Talmud, "Ethics of the Fathers"

The Final Words of Moses—Kind of, Almost

*Moses' final words are prophecy of the nation's future. His prophecy
has seven aspects. Each has come true.*

1. Exile and Worldwide Dispersion

*I appoint heaven and earth as witnesses for you today
that you will be cut off quickly from the land you are crossing the
Jordan to acquire ... God shall scatter you among the peoples and you
shall be left few in number among the nations where God will lead you.*

(Deuteronomy 4:26-27; pp. 963-965)

The Children of Israel have been dispersed to the four corners
of the Earth. Today there are synagogues in Alaska, Nairobi,
Sydney, Hong Kong, and Wichita. The dispersion of the
Israelites has been so widespread and continual, it has earned
them the nickname, "the wandering Jews."

2. Continual Persecution

*Among those nations [where you are scattered] you will find no
respite and no rest for your foot. There, God will make you
cowardly ... and make life hopeless. You will live in constant suspense.
Day and night you will be terrified, never sure of your existence. In the
morning you will say, 'If only it were night,' and in the evening you
will say, 'If only it were morning!' Such will be the dread that your
heart will feel, and the sights that your eyes will see.*

(Deuteronomy 28:65-67; pp. 1083-1085)

The following places expelled the Jews:

555 B.C.E.	Israel (Ten Tribes exiled by Assyria.)		1394 C.E.	Germany
			1394 C.E.	France
423 B.C.E.	Israel (First Temple destroyed by the Babylonians; the Jews brought to Babylon in captivity.)		1422 C.E.	Austria
			1424 C.E.	Fribourg and Zurich
			1426 C.E.	Cologne
			1432 C.E.	Savory
			1438 C.E.	Mainz
135 C.E.	Israel (Second Temple destroyed by Rome; the Jews expelled from Israel.)		1439 C.E.	Augsburg
			1456 C.E.	Bavaria
			1453 C.E.	Franconia
			1453 C.E.	Breslau
250 C.E.	Carthage		1454 C.E.	Wurzburg
415 C.E.	Alexandria		1485 C.E.	Vincenza, Italy
554 C.E.	Clement, France		1492 C.E.	Spain (Most Sephardic Jews are descendants of those expelled from Spain at this time.)
561 C.E.	Uzes, France			
612 C.E.	Visigoth, France			
642 C.E.	Visigothic Empire			
855 C.E.	Italy			
876 C.E.	Sense		1495 C.E.	Lithuania
1012 C.E.	Mayence		1497 C.E.	Portugal
1181 C.E.	France		1499 C.E.	Germany
1290 C.E.	England (Remember "Richard the Lionhearted?" He is most notable in Jewish history for burning alive the Jews of York.)		1514 C.E.	Strasbourg
			1519 C.E.	Regensburg
			1540 C.E.	Naples
			1542 C.E.	Bohemia
			1550 C.E.	Genoa
			1551 C.E.	Bavaria
			1555 C.E.	Pesaro
1306 C.E.	France		1559 C.E.	Austria
1348 C.E.	Switzerland		1561 C.E.	Prague
1348 C.E.	Alsace		1567 C.E.	Wurzburg
1349 C.E.	Hungary		1569 C.E.	Papal States
1388 C.E.	Strasbourg		1571 C.E.	Brandenburg

1582 C.E.	Netherlands
1593 C.E.	Bradenburg / Brunswick
1597 C.E.	Cremona, Pavia and Lodi
1614 C.E.	Frankfurt
1615 C.E.	Worms
1619 C.E.	Worms
1619 C.E.	Kiev
1649 C.E.	Ukraine
1649 C.E.	Hamburg
1654 C.E.	Little Russia (The persecutions of this period in Russia are known as the Chmielnitzki Massacres.)
1656 C.E.	Lithuania
1669 C.E.	Oran
1670 C.E.	Vienna
1712 C.E.	Sandomir
1727 C.E.	Russia
1738 C.E.	Wuremburg
1740 C.E.	Little Russia
1744 C.E.	Bohemia
1744 C.E.	Livonia
1745 C.E.	Moravia
1753 C.E.	Kovad, Lithuania
1761 C.E.	Bordeaux
1772 C.E.	Pale of Settlement, Russia
1775 C.E.	Warsaw
1789 C.E.	Alsace
1804 C.E.	Russian Villages

1808 C.E.	Russian Countryside
1815 C.E.	Lubeck and Bremen
1815 C.E.	Franconia, Swabia, and Bavaria
1820 C.E.	Bremes
1843 C.E.	Prussian and Russian Austrian Border
1862 C.E.	American territory under jurisdiction of General Grant.
1866 C.E.	Galazt, Romania
1919 C.E.	Bavaria
1939 C.E.	Europe (Holocaust)
1948 C.E.	Aden, Algeria, Iraq, Syria, Yemen

In addition to expulsion, Jews have frequently been subject to forced conversion, invidious taxation, restriction upon ownership of property, vicious libel, and murder.

Voltaire, the philosopher of the French Enlightenment, wrote:

We find in Jews only an ignorant and barbarous people, who have long united the most sordid avarice with the most detestable superstition and the most invincible hatred for every people by whom they are tolerated and enriched. Still, we ought not to burn them. (That was the enlightened part.)

Throughout the Middle Ages Jews were commonly accused of poisoning wells, and the belief endures that Jews plot to dominate and destroy the non-Jewish world. (<u>The Protocols of the Elders of Zion</u> is the classic exposition of this idea.)

The belief that Jews murder Christian children and drink their blood or bake it in matzos is another old standard. (Commemoration of the putative ritual murder of Simon of Trent remains a holiday celebrated in Italy on March 23. When a child disappeared in Minnesota in 1990, posters appeared suggesting that Jews had murdered him to drink his blood.)

And then, of course, there's the story that the Jews killed God. Lenny Bruce came clean on that one.

It's true we killed him. It was one of those parties that got out of hand. We killed him because he wouldn't become a doctor.

3. <u>Few in Number</u>

> *You shall remain few in number among the nations*
> *where God shall lead you.*
>
> (Deuteronomy 28:62; p. 1083)

In the past 2,000 years, the Jewish Population has grown from 6 to 13 million (<u>Carta Atlas</u>). Over a roughly comparable period, the Chinese population has gone from 13 million to over 1 billion (<u>Encyclopedia Britannica</u>).

A friend of mine points out that the most recent Chinese census contained a statistical error of plus or minus 50 million, which means there are five times as many people lost in China as there are Jews in all the world.

4. <u>Light Unto the Nations</u>

You shall become a blessing. And I will bless those who bless you, and curse those who curse you. Through you all the communities of the earth shall be blessed.

(Genesis 12:2-3; p. 55)

To [the Jews] we owe the idea of equality before the law, both divine and human, of the sanctity of life and the dignity of the human person, of the individual conscience, and so of personal redemption; of the collective conscience and so of social responsibility; of peace as an abstract ideal and of love as the foundation of justice, and many other items which constitute the basic moral furniture of the human mind. Without the Jew, it might have been a much emptier place.

Paul Johnson, History of the Jews

The Jew is that sacred being who has brought down from heaven the everlasting fire and has illuminated with it the entire world. He is the religious source, spring and fountain out of which all the rest of the peoples have

> *drawn their beliefs and their religions ... The Jew is the pioneer of civilization ...*
>
> Leo Tolstoy, What is a Jew
>
> *I will insist that the Hebrews have done more to civilize men than any other nation. If I were an atheist and believed in blind eternal fate, I should still believe that fate had ordained the Jews to be the most essential instrument for civilizing the nations ... They are the most glorious Nation that ever inhabited this earth ... [having] influenced the affairs of Mankind more, and more happily than any other nation, ancient or modern.*
>
> From a letter written by John Adams, second president of the United States, 1806.

5. The Land of Israel will remain barren and desolate until the Children of Israel return from exile

> *Future generations—your own descendants who will arise after you, as well as the foreigners who will come from distant lands—shall see the calamities of this land and the ills with which God has struck it.*
> *Sulfur and salt has burned all its soil.*
> *Nothing can be planted and nothing can grow—not even a blade of grass ...*
> *All the nations will ask, "Why did God do this to the land? What was the reason for this great display of anger?"*

> *They shall answer, "It is because they abandoned the covenant*
> *that God, Lord of their fathers, made with them when*
> *He brought them out of Egypt."*
>
> (Deuteronomy 29:21-24; p. 1089)

After the Roman expulsion of Jews from Israel, the Land was barren for nearly 2,000 years.

Mark Twain described it this way:

> *We traversed some miles of desolate country whose soil is rich enough but is given wholly to weeds—a silent, mournful expanse … A desolation is here that not even imagination can grace with the pomp of life and action. We never saw a human being on the whole route. We pressed on toward the goal of our crusade, renowned Jerusalem. The further we went the hotter the sun got and the more rocky and bare, repulsive and dreary the landscape became … There was hardly a tree or a shrub anywhere. Even the olive and the cactus, those fast friends of a worthless soil, had almost deserted the country. No landscape exists that is more tiresome to the eye than that which bounds the approaches to Jerusalem … Jerusalem is mournful, dreary and lifeless. I would not desire to live here. It is a hopeless, dreary, heartbroken land … Palestine sits in sackcloth and ashes. Over it broods the spell of a curse that has withered its fields and fettered its energies … Palestine is desolate and unlovely. And why should it be otherwise? Can the curse of the Deity beautify a land?* (The Innocents Abroad or The New Pilgrim's Progress)

But as Jews return to Israel in our century, the ground has once again become fertile.

6. Return to the Land

> *And the Lord your God shall return you from your captivity,*
> *and have compassion upon you; He shall return*

and gather you from among all the nations …
And the Lord your God will bring you into the land
that your fathers inherited. You will acquire it,
and He will make you even more prosperous
and numerous than your fathers.

(Deuteronomy 30:3-5; p. 1091)

The prophesied return of Jews to their homeland began with small groups from Eastern Europe in the late eighteenth century. Since then millions of immigrants have come from 140 countries around the world. Six hundred thousand arrived from Arab lands following the establishment of Israel in 1948 (including Jews living in exile in Yemen since the destruction of the first Temple in 3338, 423 B.C.E.). In recent decades Jews have returned home from exile in Ethiopia and from the lands of the former Soviet Union.

7. The Eternal Nation

I will establish My covenant between Me and you and your
descendants after you throughout their generations, an eternal
covenant, to be your God and the God of your descendants after you.

(Genesis 17:7; p. 73)

Even while they are in the land of their enemies,
I will not reject or obliterate them, lest I break my covenant
with them by destroying them, for I am the Lord their God.
I will remember them because of the covenant I made with their
original ancestors, whom I brought out of the land of Egypt
in the sight of the nations, so that I might be their God.

(Leviticus 26:44-45; p. 717)

I quote Mark Twain again:

If the statistics are right, the Jews constitute but one percent of the human race. It suggests a nebulous dim puff of star dust lost in the blaze of the Milky Way. Properly the Jew ought hardly to be heard of; but he is heard of, [and] has always been heard of ...

The Egyptian, the Babylonian, and the Persian rose, filled the planet with sound and splendor, and then faded to dream-stuff and passed away; the Greek and the Roman followed, and made a vast noise, and they are gone; other people have sprung up and held their torch high for a time, but it burned out, and they sit in twilight now, or have vanished. The Jew saw them all, beat them all, and is now what he always was, exhibiting no decadence, no infirmities of age, no weakening of his parts, no slowing of his energies, no dulling of his alert and aggressive mind.

All things are mortal but the Jew; all other forces pass, but he remains. What is the secret of his immortality? (Concerning the Jews)

Writing in the New York Review of Books, the historian Gary Wills considers different explanations for the anomalies of Jewish history. Was it good genes, he asks? Was it moral sensitivity, social solidarity, or ancestral loyalties? Was it self-fulfilling prophecy? All explanations, he concludes, are inadequate, save one:

"Something very strange did indeed happen to the Jews in history. It was God."

APPENDICES

I.   **Who's Who In the Bible:**
           A partial cast of biblical characters.
           (In order of appearance).

II.   **I'm Glad You Asked:**
           Thirty-two frequently asked questions
            about the Bible, religion and Judaism.

III.   **Flowing With Milk and Honey:**
           Famous Biblical phrases and what
           they really mean.

IV.   **When Did You Say This All Happened:**
           Timelines for the historically
           clueless but curious.

WHO'S WHO IN THE BIBLE

Partial Cast Of Characters (In order of appearance)

God   Author and editor of our lives. Creator of the Universe, supervisor of all creation, sustainer of all existence. Was, is, will be. Infinite, incorporeal. Outside of time—created time. Outside of space—created space. Loves us. Wants our good. Set the world in motion to accomplish same. The Big Cheese. The Boss.

Adam   First man, born on sixth day of creation—died 930 years later (low fat diet, didn't smoke, exercised regularly). Married Eve. CEO of Garden of Eden until hostile takeover by Snake. Ate from Tree of Knowledge (big mistake). Blamed his wife (bigger mistake). Forced to work for a living after expulsion from the Garden. Not Jewish.

Eve   First woman, created from Adam's rib. Seduced by Snake. Ate from Tree. Gave fruit to Adam. As punishment, forced to suffer pain of childbirth and the aggravation of raising adolescents. Mother of Cain, Able, Seth.

Snake   Very, very mean. Created by God to tempt Adam and Eve. What's his cut? Just likes being bad. Walked upright and talked. Lost legs after he seduced Adam and Eve, forced to eat dust.

Cain   Firstborn of Adam and Eve. Farmer. Name means "possession," like "mine—don't touch." Killed brother, killed by great-grandson. After banishment for murder, went into real estate development. Not a happy camper.

Abel   Second son of Adam and Eve. Naïve idealist. Name means "emptiness." Failure to fight back led to his murder by Cain.

Seth   Third son of Adam and Eve. Ancestor of Noah and everyone else. Born after death of Cain and Abel.

Noah   Built large boat. Lived through flood with wife, sons: Shem, Ham, Yefes. Planted world's first vineyard. Dysfunctional family. Not Jewish.

Shem   Firstborn of Noah. Name means "name." Descendants are "Shemites," hence anti-Shemitism.

Ham   Second son of Noah. Name means "hot," as in passionate. Tradition identifies him as the ancestor of Africa.

Yefes   Third son of Noah. Tradition identifies him as the ancestor of the Europeans in general and of the Greeks in particular. Grecian emphasis on aesthetics derives from Yefes, whose name means "beauty."

Abraham First Jew. Made a covenant with God. Two sons: Isaac from his wife, Sara, and Ishmael, from Sara's servant, Hagar. First to recognize the path to God is through kindness to other people.

Sarah   Wife of Abraham, mother of Isaac. Infertile for many years. Miraculously bore child in her nineties. Very wise.

Hagar   Daughter of Egyptian Pharaoh. Servant to Abraham and Sarah. Given by Sarah to Abraham to beget children. In words of John Lennon, asked to explain why he had 20 Rolls Royces: "At the time it seemed to make sense." Known also as Ketura. Married Abraham after the death of Sarah.

Lot   Sleazebag nephew of Abraham and Sarah. Got rich, bought condo in Sodom, had relations with daughters. Only nice thing to say is he had to get drunk first.

Mrs. Lot She and Lot deserved each other. Ambivalent about leaving Sodom. Turned to a pillar of salt.

Isaac   Son of Abraham and Sarah. Name means "laughter." Two sons: Jacob and Esau. Embodiment of justice and righteousness. Detached parenting style led to damaging consequences.

Ishmael   Name means "God has heard." Ancestor of the Arabs. In the words of God, a *vilde chaya*, "a wild animal." Wrong kid to bring to a china shop.

Rebecca   Wife of Isaac. Married young against her family's wishes, because of determination to become attached to the Jewish People. Barren for many years. Mother of Jacob and Esau.

Jacob   Son of Isaac and Rebecca. Name means "crafty." After wrestling with an angel, name changed to Israel, "prince of God." Unique perfection of character makes him the eponymous "father of the Jewish People," viz. "The Children of Israel. Twelve sons and one daughter.

Esau   Son of Isaac and Rebecca. Brother of Jacob. Man's man. Murderer, adulterer. Potential for greatness defeated by undisciplined appetites. For enjoyment of blood-sports known as Edom, "the red one." Ancestor of Rome. Quintessential antagonist to the mission of the Children of Israel.

Leah   Wife of Jacob. Mother of Reuben, Shimon, Levi, Judah, Issachar, Zevulun, and Dina.

Rachel   Wife of Jacob. Like Sarah and Rebecca infertile for many years. Mother of Joseph and Benjamin. Died giving birth to Benjamin, hence his name, literally, "son of my pain." Buried at Bethlehem, on the road the Children of Israel would tread into exile. In words of the prophets, her tears at their expulsion lead to their redemption.

Zilpah   Servant of Leah, given by her to Jacob to propagate children. Bore Gad, "good fortune," and Asher, "happy."

Bilhah   Servant of Rachel, given by her to Jacob to propagate children. Bore Dan, "(God) has judged me, and Naphtali, "divine struggle."

Twelve Tribes   Reuben, Shimon, Levi, Judah, Issachar, Zevulun, Dan, Gad, Asher, Naphtali, Joseph, Benjamin—Children of Jacob and his wives: Rachel, Leah, Bilhah, and Zilpah—Literally, "The Children of Israel," embodying within themselves the entirety of the prospective nation, in both its strengths and its weaknesses.

Dina   Daughter of Jacob and Leah. Raped by Shechem, gave birth to daughter, Asnas, who later married Joseph.

Moses   Great-grandson of Jacob, through Levi. Hidden as a baby in a basket. Found and raised by the daughter of the Pharaoh. Lisp and lack of photogenic charisma destroyed chance as local news anchorman, but in words of Shakespeare, "greatness was thrust upon him." Led Children of Israel out of slavery and gave them the Bible at God's command. The *manna* which miraculously sustained the Jews in the desert is attributed to Moses' merit. Barred from entering the land of Israel, but permitted to see it before death (whence came the words of Martin Luther King, "I've been to the mountaintop. I've seen the Promised Land"). Known as *Moshe Rabbeinu*, "Moses our Teacher."

Aharon   Brother of Moses and Miriam. First high priest of the Children of Israel. His descendants are the *cohanim*, the nation's priests. The Pillar of Fire and the Cloud of Glory, which protected and guided the Children of Israel in the desert, are attributed to his merit.

Pharaoh Arch-villain. Referred to as "the crocodile." Embodiment of arrogance and power. Set himself in opposition to God and paid for it big time.

Miriam   Sister of Moses and Aharon. One of the "Hebrew midwives," whose heroic disobedience frustrated Pharaoh's attempt to destroy the Children of Israel. The Talmud attributes the miraculous well, which sustained the Israelites in the desert, to her merit.

Korach   Great teacher and leader of the Children of Israel. Overwhelming ambition led to his destruction. Swallowed alive by the ground.

Bilaam   (Non-Jewish) prophet. Tried to curse the Children of Israel. "Dissed" by a talking donkey.

I'M GLAD YOU ASKED

Thirty-Two Frequently Asked Questions About the Bible, Religion And Judaism

People have many questions about the Bible. Some are asked innocently, while others reveal the belief that religion is irrelevant and irrational, and religious people slimy hypocrites. (Imagine what this does for my self-esteem.) When people preface a question by calling me "Rabbi," it's almost always a synonym for "idiot," as in, "but Rabbi, hasn't science proved that life on earth evolved?"

Here's some of what I put up with:

Hasn't science proved that life on earth evolved?

On simple reading, the Bible's account of creation seems like some kind of Vegas routine—rabbits popping out of hats on a grand scale. On closer attention, the Bible's account is far subtler and more complex. Medieval commentators suggest the Bible actually depicts a process of gradual evolution. God created. Evolution may be how He did it.

Didn't evolution take a lot longer than six days?

The six days of creation can't be twenty-four-hour days. Light appears on the first day, but the sun and moon don't turn up until the fourth. Commentators suggest the six "days" of creation may be six epochs of creation. Each epoch may have lasted weeks, months, or like Mrs. Magwire's ninth grade math class on a hot afternoon, billions of years.

Isn't religion for people who aren't willing to think for themselves?

In most areas of knowledge, rote memorization of basic information lays the foundation for higher reasoning. You didn't discover the number system, the alphabet, the laws of grammar, arithmetic, or the postulates of geometry yourself. No doctor derives for himself the laws of organic chemistry or of pharmacology for himself. The foundation of knowledge we learn from others permits us to learn for ourselves.

The same is true with religion. The Bible states spiritual and moral postulates. Applying those principles—deciding which applies, when, and how—is the ultra-hard work of thinking that makes each of us unique.

Aren't religious people smug, self-satisfied, and dogmatic?

I think this is actually a slur and not a question, but let's try it anyway.

Because being pigheaded is easier than thinking, smug dogmatism is a human failing. Religious people are human; ergo, they are sometimes smug and dogmatic. The only antidote is being reasonable.

In the words of the philosopher Quine:

To believe something is to believe that it is true; therefore a reasonable person believes each of his beliefs to be true; yet experience has taught him to expect that some of his beliefs, he knows not which, will turn out to be false. A reasonable person believes, in short, that each of his beliefs is true and that some of them are false." (Quidditties)

What happens when the Bible conflicts with human reason? What if God tells you to do something you think is immoral—like sacrifice your son, or fling yourself into a mine field screaming, "Allah Akbar!"

The first question is whether God is really talking, if you're overly imaginative or schizophrenic. If it is God talking, then we assume God is right (it's one of the perks of the job). If you think God is wrong, it's possible you're not seeing the whole picture. Imagine, for example, watching three people pin someone to a table and cut his leg off. You need history and context to know whether you're watching surgery or torture. The story of Abraham's sacrifice of Isaac explores this very difficult question.

Who cares? So what? Why should I read this book at all?

Here's a high-class question.

Do you want to be happy? Do you want a good marriage and well-adjusted children? Do you want meaning? Is it easy to achieve these things? Show me someone who thinks life is straightforward, and I'll show you a two-year-old. For 3,300 years, people have read the Bible for insight. That suggests the Bible's answers to life's questions are worth thinking about.

I'm happy. Why should I get involved with religion?

They say you can never be too rich or too thin (which explains why many people are neurotic and their kids are anorexic). But it probably is true that you can't be too happy or too wise.

Put differently, a business that becomes complacent when things go well won't be in business very long.

How could a book that's 3,300 years old be relevant to my life?

Ever read Plato? Aristotle? Sophocles? Shakespeare? In Athens, Portland, or cyberspace, life's key challenges haven't changed much in the past several millennia. Classics are timeless whether you wear a ring in your nose, your ear, or your belly button.

Isn't the Bible sexist and patriarchal?

No.

The heart and the brain are different, but each is indispensable, and it's meaningless to ask, "Which is better?" Men and women are different—each has different strengths and different weaknesses.

Each is indispensable to a complete portrait of being human. Assuming momentarily that men and women are the same, is reproduction the only reason to marry someone of the opposite gender?

Isn't religion the cause of great suffering and violence?

Much blood has been shed in the name of religion. But history's sanguinary prize goes to secular zealots, from the French Revolution through Communism and National Socialism.

Violence actually has little to do with religion or with whatever ideological rationalization people offer for killing. It has a lot to do with the need to feel important by standing on someone else's head.

Aren't the Bible's laws restrictive and oppressive?

Great ballet dancers evince breathtaking grace. But their evident freedom is only achieved through rigorous discipline and training. So too in the realm of the soul—the grace and beauty of true moral character are not forged through sloppy good intentions. They depend on discipline, training and hard work.

Isn't the Bible authoritarian? Isn't there a conflict between religion and democracy?

The Ten Commandments are not the Ten Suggestions. On the other hand, observance under duress has no moral value. You can lead a cow with a ring in its nose. You only lead a human being by appealing to his mind. God asks us to freely submit to His authority.

Doesn't religion just fill people with guilt?

The Bible actually considers guilt a cheap alternative to real regret and change. If you're walking down the street and discover you have a hole in your pocket don't stand around feeling guilty. Transfer any remaining coins to the other pocket, and then go on. When you get home, sew up the pocket. Regret and change are useful. Guilt is pointless and destructive.

Why do religious people think they're better than other people?

See "Aren't religious people smug, self-satisfied, and dogmatic."

Believing you own the revealed word of God does lead to complacency and arrogance. Religious people need to work extra hard at being humble.

Why are religious people so intolerant?

Tolerance means assuming the people you disagree with are honest and well meaning. It doesn't mean all opinions have equal merit or that no one is right. As Dorothy Parker said, "If two people agree, one of them is unnecessary."

It is also crucial to distinguish between loving people and loving all their actions or beliefs.

Rabbi Aryeh Levin lived in Israel during the British Mandate. One Shabbat, he was walking in the streets of Jerusalem when a secular Israeli came toward him, smoking a cigarette.

"My master," said Reb Aryeh, "it's prohibited to smoke on Shabbat."

"I'm not Jewish," said the Israeli, "I'm a goy!"

"Oh my son, don't say that," said Reb Aryeh. "I love you as my own child."

The Israeli paused.

"The Rabbi doesn't want me to smoke? I'll put it out."

"Don't put it out," said Reb Aryeh, "just put it down."

"I can't tell the Rabbi I'll never again smoke on Shabbat," said the Israeli, "but this Shabbat, I won't smoke."

If I'm not perfect, does that mean I'm going to hell? Alternatively, if I can't keep all the Bible's commandments, is it hypocritical to keep any of them?

Here's a guy with a real head case:

The doctor tells him that his health is lousy. "Quit smoking," he says. "Cut down on fat. Exercise. Lose weight."

"I can't do all that," he says, "so what's the point of trying?" He goes out and has a double pastrami cheese melt and washes it down with chewing tobacco.

A sensible guy says, "Doctor, I hear what you're saying. I may not do everything you suggest, but I'll do the best I can."

For the good we do, we'll get reward. For the bad we do, we'll pay a price. Do your best.

What is the Bible's view of abortion?

The Bible permits killing an unborn child when the mother's life is threatened, whether physically or by extremely severe emotional trauma. (The discovery she is carrying a Tay-Sachs child for example, might be grounds for abortion.). Absent these circumstances, the Bible views abortion as murder.

Though the miracles of language can turn a baby into a fetus, abortion is not an acceptable form of birth control.

What's really wrong with shrimp? Weren't those laws made because of health?

The commandments sometimes have physical side benefits, but in traditional belief, this is "just the gravy." The real benefit of God's commandments is spiritual. In case of the dietary laws, this may mean learning boundaries for our appetites, or it may mean discovering we can sanctify the act of eating.

Does the Bible think everyone has to be a rabbi/priest/minister?

No.

If the Bible is so great, why have so many people turned away from it?

Lousy education.

What makes me special? Where do I fit in?

The rules say each of us must forge a relationship with God. Each must give to others. Each is challenged to sanctify and uplift the world.

But each of us has unique assets, and each contributes something unique to the vision of God's presence in the world. Harness your skill-set to the task, and give it all you've got.

What's the meaning of life?

God created us to have pleasure. Now go study what that means.

What difference does it make that there's a God?

It means you're not an animated hunk of meat and fat on a rock orbiting the sun. It means you're more than top predator on the food chain.

If there's a God, why do good people suffer? In general, why isn't God's presence more obvious?

Inherited wealth is a mixed blessing. Our own achievements are the ones we value most. God is concealed in the world so we can find Him.

Suffering forces us to think more deeply about what really matters. Speaking personally, the most important things I know, I learned through pain.

If the Jews are the chosen people, why are they so hated?

The Jews are the world's conscience. No one likes a conscience.

I went to Sunday school and hated it. Why should I learn more now?

Kids love candy, but most gourmet pleasures are acquired tastes. This is true of wine, cheese, cigars, and coffee. Wisdom is an acquired taste.

Who or what is the Messiah?

The Messiah will be a human being descended from King David. He will unite the Jewish People and lead them back to their relationship with God and Torah. When that occurs, the nations of the world will also acknowledge the truth of God's Law, and then the world will live in peace. (This is the meaning of the prophecy that the wolf will lie down with the lamb.)

What's the difference between Judaism, Christianity, and Islam? Aren't they all based on the Bible?

Skateboards, tanks and racing cars are all based on wheels. They're radically different forms of transportation.

Isn't it enough to be a good person? Why do you have to believe in God?

The rudiments of moral goodness are within us. But it takes more than natural ability to get into the NBA. It takes instruction and training. God's instructions and God's assistance help us to become great.

Is the Bible only for Jews?

No.

The Bible gives non-Jews seven commandments (the Noachide commandments, which establish the basis for a lawful and just society). The Bible gives Jews 613 commandments, relating to the sanctification of every aspect of life. Judaism isn't a closed club of gender or of race. Anyone who wants to share that mission is welcome to join.

Does the Bible believe in life after death?

Yes.

Think of the soul as a lens. Every act—every choice—either polishes the lens or scratches it. When the body dies, the soul remains. If we burnish the soul's lens, the soul's vision of God is glorious and beautiful. That is heaven. If we scratch the lens and occlude it, we obscure the soul's vision forever. The pain of that loss is hell.

Can you read the Bible if you don't believe in God?

If every time the Bible says "God said … " your response is "I don't believe that," you won't get much from the experience. You'll find it more meaningful to momentarily suspend belief. Ask yourself, "If there were a God, why would He say this?"

FLOWING WITH MILK AND HONEY

Famous Biblical Phrases And What They Really Mean

Let there be light (Genesis 1:3, p. 5)

Hey! Who likes to read in the dark? Besides, the light God's speaking of is much more than wattage. The light referred to is illumination—the hints of holiness and transcendence that bring meaning to our lives.

It isn't good for man to be alone (Genesis 2:18; p. 13)

God's reason for creating Eve. God wasn't concerned how mankind would reproduce. Rather, man alone is sterile, not just physically, but emotionally and spiritually as well. The journey toward God starts with the relationship between a man and his wife.

Adam's rib (Genesis 2:21; p. 15)

The building block of Eve's creation. Man and woman make up the fullness of what we call human. The rib is concealed—women nurture the private interior dimension of our experience. The skeleton gives structure and support—women provide the structure that gives stability to the family. (This thought is echoed by the Jewish custom for a bride to circle the groom under the wedding canopy. *"Isha tisovev gever,"* says the Talmud, "a woman surrounds a man." She creates the definition and boundaries of home which permit him to relate effectively to the world around him.)

By the sweat of your brow you will eat bread (Genesis 3:19; p. 19)

God's punishment of Adam after he and Eve eat from the Tree of Knowledge. Colloquially, "go get a job." Of your seventy allotted years, deduct the twenty-three spent sleeping and the eleven and a half spent bathing and eating. That leaves thirty-six. Of those, twenty-three (minimum) will be spent working, which leaves just thirteen for loving, dreaming, thinking, planning, growing, singing, dancing, reading. That's a curse.

You are dust and to dust you will return (Genesis 3:19; p. 19)

Nothing focuses the mind like the prospect of being shot in the morning. Death is a blessing because it forces us to distinguish between the lasting and meaningful and the trivial and fleeting. (Ever heard someone eulogized for driving the latest car?) Death wasn't part of the original plan, but after Adam and Eve ate from the Tree of Knowledge, God decided man needs the discipline of a final exam.

Am I my brother's keeper? (Genesis 4:9; p. 21)

Cain's evasion of responsibility for killing Abel. He implied the guilt was actually God's for failing to prevent the murder from taking place. See: "Where was God during the Holocaust?" See also the definition of *chutzpah*: The man who kills his parents and throws himself on the court's mercy because he's an orphan.

A land flowing with milk and honey (Exodus 3:17; p. 305)

"Milk" means goat milk, and "honey" means date honey. Israel is a supremely good land, with otherworldly beauty. Elsewhere, God is a theory, but in Israel, God is a reality.

Let my people go (Exodus 7:16; p. 327)

God's message to Pharaoh, delivered through Moses. Particularly stirring when delivered in deep bass by Paul Robeson. People forget the second half, namely: "Let my people go that they may serve me." Freedom is not an end. It's a means. Freedom from Egypt permits the Israelites to serve God more fully.

On the wings of eagles (Exodus 19:4; p. 403)

How God took the Israelites out of Egypt. It means they went out with grandeur, dignity, and power.

An eye for an eye and a tooth for a tooth (Exodus 21:24; p. 423)

The basic principle of justice, known as "the law of talon." Punishment is only just when it's commensurate with the crime. In actual practice, Biblical courts didn't remove eyes or teeth, but calculated their monetary value and assigned that amount as damages. Mothers voice the law of talon when they say, "One day your children will drive you crazy, just like you're driving me crazy!"

A stiff-necked people (Exodus 33:5; p. 503)

Stubborn and resistant to reproof—God's description of the Israelites' character. By and large, it's not complimentary, though the upside is that words engraved in stone last longer than words engraved in butter.

The scapegoat (Leviticus 16:6-11; p. 639)

On Yom Kippur, the High Priest set aside two identical goats. He offered one as a sacrifice in the Temple. Leaning his hands on the head of the other, he listed the Israelites' mistakes and then threw the goat over a cliff. The two goats dramatize the miracle of free will: Outwardly identical—one achieves calumny, the other sanctity. The explanation for what we make of our lives is not in our circumstances. It's in our choices.

Don't put a stumbling block before the blind (Leviticus 19:14; p. 661)

Don't tell someone to do something you know they shouldn't do. E.g., "Hey Tommy! Want to have some fun? Let's set off the fire alarm and run away!"

Love your neighbor as yourself (Leviticus 19:18; p. 661)

It's an obligation to love other people. At a minimum, you're obligated to act like you love them. (If you do that, you eventually will love them.)

Treat others the way you'd like them to treat you. In Bible-speak, "Do unto others as you would have them do unto you."

Proclaim freedom throughout the land (Leviticus 25:10; p. 699)

The Biblical calendar is broken into fifty-year cycles. The fiftieth year is called the Jubilee. In the Jubilee year a proclamation sets all slaves free. In The Gifts of the Jews, Thomas Cahill says Jews taught the world to yearn for freedom.

Man does not live by bread alone (Deuteronomy 8:3; p. 983)

Cats eat, drink, and sleep in the sun. Cows ruminate, which means they spend more time chewing. Man needs more. He needs meaning. The second half of the verse is oft-forgotten. "Man does not live by bread alone. He lives by the word of God."

Justice, justice you shall pursue (Deuteronomy 16:20; p. 1025)

Justice is good. It isn't enough to hope for it in a warm, fuzzy kind of way. You have to run after it and work for it as you'd run for silver and for gold.

There is nothing new under the sun

This is actually not from the Five Books of Moses, but from the Book of Ecclesiastes, written by King Solomon. Run here. Run there. Buy this. Buy that. Ads pretend the right product or vacation will change your life. But it's a dream. If you aren't happy, nothing outside will do it for you. You want something truly new and rewarding? Look to the realm of the spirit. That's above the sun.

WHEN DID YOU SAY THIS ALL HAPPENED?

Timelines For The Historically Clueless But Curious

Timeline of Major Biblical Events
Overview of Early Jewish and World History

Date	Person	Biblical Event	World Event
0/3761 BCE	Adam and Eve	Eat from tree	Creation
0/3761 BCE	Cain and Abel	First murder	Pre-History
1436/2325 BCE	Noah's family	Flood	Epic of Gilgamesh
1996/1765 BCE	Shem	Tower of Babel	Egyptian papyrus
2080/1671 BCE	Abraham & Sarah	Covenant w/God	European Bronze Age
2048/1713 BCE	Isaac	Circumcision	Stonehenge
2085/1676 BCE	Isaac & Ishmael	Non-sacrafice of Isaac	Paganism
2108/1653 BCE	Jacob's family	Jacob & Esau	India: Upanishad
2199/1562 BCE	Twelve Tribes	Joseph & brothers	Egyptian dynasty
2332/1428 BCE	Pharoah	Slavery in Egypt	Early Chinese dynasties
2448/1312 BCE	Moses	Exodus & Mt. Sinai	Mycenaean Greece
2488/1272 BCE	Joshua	Jews enter Israel	King Tut mummified

Timeline of Major Jewish and World Events
Overview of Post Biblical Jewish History

Date	Jewish History	World History
2080/1671 BCE	Abraham & Sarah	European Bronze Age
2448/1312 BCE	Exodus & Torah at Mt. Sinai	Mycenaean Greece
2488/1272 BCE	Joshua & Jews enter Israel	King Tut/ Trojan War
2881/880 BCE	Saul is first King of Israel	Phoenicians settle Cyprus
2884/877 BCE	King David/ Book of Psalms	Homer/ Iliad & Odyssey
2935/825 BCE	First Temple built in Jerusalem	Rise of Carthage
2964/796 BCE	Israel splits into Judah & Israel	Apollo and the Oracle at Delphi
3206/555 BCE	Assyrians exile the Ten Tribes	Gautama the Buddah/ Confucius
3338/422 BCE	Babylonians destroy First Temple	Socrates and Plato
3405/355 BCE	Mordecai, Esther & Purim	Persian Empire/First wall in China
3408/352 BCE	Second Temple built	Roman Republic
3597/165 BCE	Maccabees & Chanukah miracle	Rome defeats Macedon
3830/70 BCE	Romans destroy Second Temple	Mayan civilization
3979/219 CE	Yehuda Hanasi compiles Mishna	Early Christianity
4260/500	Babylonian Talmud compiled	Holy Roman Empire
4382/622	Era of Geonic sages	Mohammad flees Mecca
4527/767	Karaite sect rejects Oral Law	Middle (Dark) Ages/ Charlemagne
4856/1096	Rashi's commentary on Bible	First Crusades
4931/1171	Maimonides/ Mishna Torah	Saladin defeats Egypt
5252/1492	Jews expelled from Spain	Spain defeats Moors/Columbus sails
5532/1772	Rise of Chassidism	Boston/ colonies demand rights
5657/1897	Herzl & First Zionist Congress	Spanish American War (1898)
5698/1939	Holocaust/ 6,000,000 murdered	World War II
5708/1948	Rebirth of Israel	Gandhi assasinated/Truman elected
5727/1967	Six-Day War/ Jerusalem reunified	Vietnam War
5750/1990	Exodus of Russian Jews to Israel	Nobel Prize to Gorbachev

My Thoughts And Questions About the Bible

My Thoughts And Questions About the Bible

My Thoughts And Questions About the Bible

Nachum Braverman
Seminars and Lectures
(310) 278-8672

"Nachum radiates an enthusiasm to share his knowledge and to promote an introspective thought process. He is truly a brilliant teacher."
Charles E. Hurwitz, Chairman, President & CEO
MAXXAM Inc.

"Nachum takes traditional Jewish wisdom and makes it come alive. I wish his insights and intellectual energy could be packaged and delivered to each and every human being."
J. Morton Davis, Chairman of the Board
D.H. Blair Investment Banking Corp.

"If anyone can teach you how to uncover the meaning you want in life, it's Nachum Braverman. He is not only a wonderful teacher, he genuinely cares about his students."
Cathy Chessler, PR & Marketing Consultant

"Nachum Braverman is one of the most provocative and inspiring teachers in the Jewish world today."
David Wilstein, Past General Chairman, United
Jewish Fund of Los Angeles and President, Realtech
Leasing and Management

"An exceptionally compassionate teacher. He taught my husband and I how to have a productive, meaningful fight."
Susan Weintraub, Homemaker

"Studying with Nachum is an exhilirating, challenging, provocative, intriguing, compelling, transforming experience."
Lou Rudolph, ABC Executive Producer of Roots and Rich Man, Poor Man

Also by Nachum Braverman

THE DEATH OF CUPID
Reclaiming the Wisdom of Love, Dating, Romance and Marriage

"An insightful guide to discovering the beautifully deep potential of marriage."
John Gray, Ph.D.,author of Men Are From Mars, Women Are From Venus

"I wish I had this book 25 years ago. The Death of Cupid is a must for anyone who wants to stay happily married."
Larry King

"Wise,terse and powerful. The Death of Cupid is a provocative and valuable piece of work that will not only change minds—it can change people's lives."
Michael Medved,PBS Film Critic, author Hollywood Vs America. Dr. Diane Medved, author The Case Against Divorce and co-author The American Family.

"The Death of Cupid clearly describes the steps that are necessary to find a loving and satisfying relationship."
Janice D. Bennett, Ph.D. Acting Clinical Director of the Marpeh Clinic, affiliated with the Albert Einstein College of Medicine and a co-founder of workshops on successful dating.

"Never underestimate the wisdom of the ancients, which is captured so well in this book."
Mortimer B. Zuckerman, Chairman, U.S. News & World Report, The Atlantic Monthly, The Daily News

✦

Available at better booksellers nationwide or
directly from the publisher.

✦

To Order Call: (410)653-0300 / (800) 538-4284

LEVIATHAN PRESS
BOOKS THAT MAKE A DIFFERENCE

To Order Books From Leviathan Press, Call: (410) 653-0300 or (800) 538-4284

New 1998 Publication

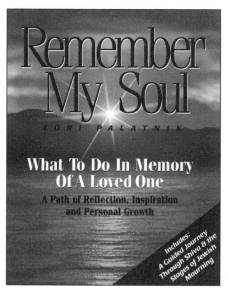

Remember My Soul
WHAT TO DO IN MEMORY OF A LOVED ONE

A Path of Reflection, Inspiration and
Personal Growth

*Includes: A Guided Journey Through Shiva
and the Stages of Jewish Mourning*

by Lori Palatnik

*Dear Lori, As a therapist and, as a mourner,
I related to your book in many ways. It helps
a person through the steps of mourning and,
to some degree, the acceptance of the loss and
incorporation of positive memories and lessons.*
Robbie Schwartz, Family Therapist

*Dear Lori, During the shiva for my father people were well meaning, but I was
lost within myself. After my father's death I felt a great need to do something. I
am indebted to you for giving me your book so that I could learn to do something
meaningful to me and relevant to my father's memory.*
Bob Skolnik, Engineer

*Remember My Soul teaches the bereaved to harness the rich resources of Jewish
spirituality. It demonstrates how to turn the pain of losing a dear one into a
vehicle for human wholeness.*
Rabbi E.B. Freedman, Director of Jewish Hospice Services,
Hospice of Michigan

The Newly Revised and Expanded
Rosh Hashanah Yom Kippur Survival Kit
by Shimon Apisdorf

Bestselling recipient of a Benjamin Franklin Award

There you are; it's the middle of High Holy Day services, and frankly, you're confused. Enter—the *Rosh Hashanah Yom Kippur Survival Kit*. This book follows the order of the services and masterfully blends wisdom, humor and down-to-earth spirituality. It's like having a knowledgeable friend sitting right next to you in synagogue.

CHANUKAH
Eight Nights of Light,
Eight Gifts For The Soul
by Shimon Apisdorf
1997 Benjamin Franklin Award

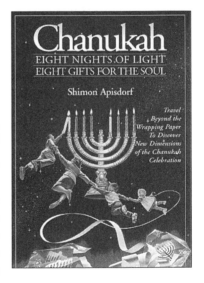

The goal of this book is to peel away the outer layers of Chanukah, the wrapping paper if you will, and reveal a profoundly rich, spiritual core to the holiday.

Chanukah is about the awesome subtleness of life. It's about the power in a diminutive flame to banish an enormous darkness. It's about the imperceptible human spark that enables us to reach far beyond our perceived limitations. It's about how little things can make a profound difference, and it's about discovering the soul in the flame, the soul in everyday life and the power of the soul in Jewish history.   *From the Introduction*

PASSOVER SURVIVAL KIT
by Shimon Apisdorf

This internationally acclaimed bestseller, serves as a friendly gateway through which you will enter the world of Passover and see it as you have never seen it before. The Passover Survival Kit enables you to experience one of the centerpieces of Jewish life as insightful, thought-provoking and relevant to issues of personal growth and the everyday challenges of life. This book stands on its own and also serves as a companion volume to *The Survival Kit Family Haggadah.*

THE SURVIVAL KIT FAMILY HAGGADAH
by Shimon Apisdorf

The only Haggadah in the world… **Featuring** the Matzahbrei Family. A loveable family of matzah people that guide you and your family through a delightful, insightful, spiritual and fun seder. **Featuring** the "talking Haggadah." A revolutionary translation. Never again will you read a paragraph in the Haggadah and say, "Huh, what's that supposed to mean?"
Written as a companion to the *Passover Survival Kit*

About the Author

Nachum Braverman studied philosophy at Yale University, and earned rabbinical ordination at Aish HaTorah College of Jewish Studies in Jerusalem. Since 1983 he has been Educational Director of Aish HaTorah for the Western Region. Together with Shimon Apisdorf he is the author of <u>The Death of Cupid: Reclaiming the Wisdom of Love, Dating, Romance, and Marriage</u>. His writings on relationships and contemporary issues have been published in many periodicals including The New York Times. Together with his wife Emuna and their children, he lives in Los Angeles.